Circle C Beginnings Activity Guide

Author: Susan K. Marlow
Activity pages created by Susan K. Marlow
(includes daily schedule)

CircleCBooks.com

Circle C Beginnings Activity Guide
© 2022-2024 by Susan K. Marlow

Study guide published by
Circle C Creations
Tonasket, WA
www.CircleCAdventures.com

Andi's Pony Trouble © 2010
Andi's Indian Summer © 2010
Andi's Fair Surprise © 2011
Andi's Scary School Days © 2011
Andi's Lonely Little Foal © 2011
Andi's Circle C Christmas © 2011
by Susan K. Marlow
Illustrated by Leslie Gammelgaard

Books published by
Kregel Publications
Grand Rapids, MI
www.kregel.com

Permission to reproduce these pages in part or in whole is granted for individual or classroom use. Not for resale.

ISBN: 978-0-9975067-1-6

Printed in the United States of America

Contents

HOW TO USE THIS GUIDE 5

*All chapter activities include **vocabulary** and **comprehension** questions,
as well as the specific, thematic topics listed in italics below:*

1. ANDI'S PONY TROUBLE

    Daily Schedule for Andi's Pony Trouble 6

    Chapters 1–3 *geography; pet care; writing activity* 7

    Chapters 4–6 *egg math; measuring Midnight* 12

    Chapters 7–9 *who am I? Help Andi find Coco maze* 17

    Chapter 10 & Peek into the Past *Andi's sugar cookies; idioms*. 20

2. ANDI'S INDIAN SUMMER

    Daily Schedule for Andi's Indian Summer 24

    Chapters 1–3 *dime novels; create a dime novel* 25

    Chapters 4–6 *creek animals; dot-to-dot mystery animal* 30

    Chapters 7–9 *Yokut word puzzle; Yokut baskets; weave a placemat* 37

    Chapter 10 & Peek into the Past *alike and different; "diligent" character trait* 40

3. ANDI'S FAIR SURPRISE

    Daily Schedule for Andi's Fair Surprise 44

    Chapters 1–3 *geography; steam trains; inside a steam engine*. 45

    Chapters 4–6 *fair math; Who am I?*. 50

    Chapters 7–10 *twenty cents; dot-to-dot prize* 55

    Chapter 10 & Peek into the Past *character ribbons; "security" character trait* . . . 57

4. ANDI'S SCARY SCHOOL DAYS

    Daily Schedule Daily Schedule for Andi's Scary School Days 62

    Chapters 1–3 *American flag; schoolroom map; "America" song* 63

    Chapters 4–6 *McGuffey reader; copy work.* 68

    Chapters 7–9 *Fun with words; schoolhouse maze.* 77

    Chapter 10 & Peek into the Past *1874 school rules; horse colors; "peaceful" trait*   80

5. ANDI'S LONELY LITTLE FOAL

    Daily Schedule for Andi's Lonely Little Foal 84

    Chapters 1–3 *geography; western idioms; foal maze* 85

    Chapters 4–6 *cowboy clothes; horse tack* 90

    Chapters 7–9 *Jesus Loves Me" song; copy work* 99

    Chapter 10 & Peek into the Past *"boldness" character trait.* 102

6. ANDI'S CIRCLE C CHRISTMAS

    Daily Schedule for Andi's Circle C Christmas 104

    Chapters 1–3 *blue-belly lizards; geography; the Presidio fort in San Francisco* 105

    Chapters 4–6 *story characters* 110

    Chapters 7–9 *What's Missing?* 113

    Chapter 10 & Peek into the Past *puzzle; Magi maze; Victorian decorations; "joyful"* 116

7. ANSWER KEYS

    Andi's Pony Trouble 122

    Andi's Indian Summer 123

    Andi's Fair Surprise 124

    Andi's Scary School Days 125

    Andi's Lonely Little Foal 126

    Andi's Circle C Christmas 127

Circle C Beginnings Activity Pages

The Circle C Beginnings books and activities guide can be used as a reading curriculum. The activities cover a wide range of historical and language arts-related topics:

- Vocabulary and reading comprehension
- Geography and map skills
- Historical topics related to the 1870s: ranching, cowboys, one-room schoolhouses, 1874 school rules, dime novels, the Yokut Indians, steam trains, state fairs, the U.S. flag, McGuffey readers, "Jesus Love Me" song origin, "America" song, the Presidio fort in San Francisco
- Math and science: egg math, tallying, Venn diagram, creek animals, blue-belly lizards, horse measuring, horse colors, pet care, steam engines
- Language arts: write or narrate, Old West idioms, create a dime novel, characters
- Character and Bible: character ribbons, character traits, Bible verses
- Crafts and "just for fun": sugar cookies, weave a placemat, mazes, dot-to-dots, Victorian Christmas decorations
- Answer key for all six books

Each book takes about 16 days to complete. The (optional) Circle C Beginnings lapbook activities stretch that to 24 days per book. It is available as an E-book or print at **CircleCAdventures.com** and covers all six books with unique learning activities not covered in this activity guide.

The books are chronological, but they are also stand-alone stories and need not be read in order. (You can read *Andi's Circle C Christmas* during the holidays, for instance.)

BONUS! Guide includes links to online video and audio enrichment hosted on the Circle C website at CircleCBooks.com/beginnings/ Safe and secure!

Susan Marlow

Schedule for Book 1: **Andi's Pony Trouble**

*indicates an optional activity found in the *Andi's Pony Trouble* lapbook.
(Lapbook activities **can be skipped** or purchased at CircleCAdventures.com)

Pony Trouble	Day 1	Day 2	Day 3	Day 4
Book	"New Words" & Chapter 1	------	Chapter 2	------
Activities	Page 7 #1-4	* Lapbook activity "About the Book" & Lapbook cover	Page 7 #5-7	* Lapbook activity Chapters 1-2
Pony Trouble	Day 5	Day 6	Day 7	Day 8
Book	Chapter 3	------	------	Chapter 4
Activities	Page 7 #8-11	Pages 8-9	Pages 10-11	Page 12 #1-4
Pony Trouble	Day 9	Day 10	Day 11	Day 12
Book	------	Chapter 5	Chapter 6	------
Activities	* Lapbook activity Chapters 3-4	Page 12 #5-9	Page 12 #10-13	* Lapbook activity Chapters 5-6
Pony Trouble	Day 13	Day 14	Day 15	Day 16
Book	------	------	Chapter 7	Chapter 8
Activities	Pages 13-14	Pages 15-16	Page 17 #1-4	Page 17 #5-7
Pony Trouble	Day 17	Day 18	Day 19	Day 20
Book	------	Chapter 9	------	Chapter 10
Activities	* Lapbook activity Chapters 7-8	Page 17 #8-11	Pages 18-19	Page 20 #1-4
Pony Trouble	Day 21	Day 22	Day 23	Day 24
Book	------	A Peek into the Past	------	------
Activities	* Lapbook activity Chapters 9-10	Page 20 #5 and Let's Write!	Pages 21-23	* Lapbook activity 5 story elements

Andi's Pony Trouble Chapters 1-3

Read the chapters and answer the questions.

Chapter 1- Andi's Great Idea

1. The <u>main character</u> is who the story is about. Who is the main character in this story? _____

2. What meal is Andi's family eating at the beginning of this chapter?

    A. breakfast   B. lunch   C. supper

3. Andi is having a birthday soon. She will be _____ years old.

4. What month is it? _____ What year is it? _____

Chapter 2- Big Enough?

5. Look at the picture on page 16. Write the names of Andi's brothers and sister: _____ _____

    _____ _____

6. What is the name of Andi's pony? _____

7. Circle the animal Andi wants more than anything!
    a puppy • a horse • a kitten

Chapter 3- Chickens and Chores

8. YES or NO (circle one)? Andi takes good care of Coco, her pony.

9. What is Andi's chore?

    A. collecting the eggs   B. cleaning her room   C. sweeping the floor

10. Henry the Eighth is a (circle one): dog • rooster • horse • hen

11. How many eggs does Andi collect from the hens? _____

New Words Chapters 1-3

Word Match- Draw a line between the words and what they mean. If you need help, look at the New Words list on page 7 in *Pony Trouble*.

cattle • a farm where people raise cattle and horses

ranch • cows

coop • pants

roundup • a place where chickens are kept

britches • when cowboys gather up the cattle to sell them

More Fun with New Words

Use the words from the word box and the clues to fill in the missing words in these sentences from chapters 1-3.

1. Andi _____ at Chad. (frowned in a mean way)

2. Pretty soon she would not be riding that _____ old pony anymore. (very, very slow)

3. Andi did not want to ride a _____ pony anymore. (used by everyone, worn out)

4. Andi _____ down on the ground. (sank, fell)

5. "Mitch can _____ four eggs at a time!" (toss in the air)

```
Word Box
juggle    pokey    slumped    hand-me-down    scowled
```

Where Does Andi Live?

Andi lives on a big cattle ranch in the state of California. She lives in 1874. That's *way* long ago! Look at the map of the United States. Can you find California? It is the long, narrow state right next to the Pacific Ocean. Color California red.

What state do you live in? _____

Color your state blue (even if you live in California).

Taking Care of Coco

Andi has to take care of Coco, her pony. Here are some of her chores:

* Brush Coco

* Give Coco water

* Make sure Coco has hay and grain

* Let Coco out in the pasture

* Ride Coco for exercise

* Check Coco's hooves for rocks and dirt

* Clean out Coco's stall

Color Andi's pony Coco, and his saddle and reins.

Taking Care of My Pet

If you do not have a pet, think of a pet you would like.

My pet is a _____

My pet's name is _____

This is what I do to take care of my pet:
_____
_____
_____
_____
_____

Draw a picture of your pet.

What Are You Afraid Of?

Andi is scared of Henry the Eighth, the big, black rooster. But Riley helps Andi. He chases the rooster.

What are *you* afraid of? Write about a time when you were afraid. What happened? Did somebody help you? You may tell your story to a parent. They can write down what you say. You may also draw a picture.

Henry the Eighth

Andi's Pony Trouble Chapters 4-6

Read the chapters and answer the questions.

Chapter 4- Riley to the Rescue

1. _____ is Andi's friend. He chases the rooster away.

2. Circle the reasons why Andi does not like Henry the Eighth:

    He chases her. • He is bigger than she is. • He pecks her.

    He gets her all wet. • He makes her spill her eggs. • He is mean.

3. Color the number of eggs Andi finds that are <u>not</u> broken.

4. YES or NO (circle one)? The ranch dogs like to eat drippy eggs.

Chapter 5- Slow-poke Pony

5. What is the name of Riley's horse? _____

6. How old is Andi's friend Riley (circle one)?   seven • eight • nine

7. What color is Coco's mane? _____

8. What color is Coco's coat (body)? _____

9. YES or NO (circle one)? After three tries, Andi gets up on Midnight.

Chapter 6- Andi's Great Idea

10. Andi does not like to trot. She wants to _____ very fast.

11. What does Riley grab onto (circle one)?   Coco's mane • Coco's reins

12. What does Coco do that makes Andi fall off?

    A. He galloped too fast.   B. He bucked her off.   C. He stopped.

13. YES or NO (circle one)? Midnight gallops away when the children fall off.

New Words Chapters 4–6

Turn back to page 7 in *Pony Trouble* and find the three words below. Write what each word means.

1. **corral** _____

   _____

2. **howdy** _____

3. **whinny** _____

New Words Riddles

Can you guess the words from the riddle clues? Use the word box for help.

4. I am buckled around a horse's head. I keep the bit in place and make sure the horse obeys. What am I? _____

5. This is what happened to Coco's mane when Andi didn't take care of him. It got all _____.

6. Coco does not like to gallop. He would rather walk or _____.

7. I am a toy. When you turn the handle music plays. Then all of a sudden I jump out and surprise you. What am I?

   _____

Word Box

trot   jack-in-the-box   bridle   tangled

Color me!

Color the Ponies

Six ponies are trotting across this page. A sentence about *Pony Trouble* is written inside each pony. If the sentence is true, color the pony. If the sentence is NOT true, draw a big X across the pony.

1. Chad saved Andi from the rooster.
2. Midnight is Riley's horse.
3. Riley is 8 years old.
4. All the eggs Andi collected broke.
5. Midnight ran away.
6. Coco galloped for a long time.

Egg Math

Collecting the eggs is Andi's chore. Can you help her solve these problems?

1. Andi collected **18** eggs. **16** eggs broke.

    How many eggs were left to give to Mother? _____ eggs

    Hint: Draw 18 eggs. Cross out 16 eggs that broke.

2. **20** hens, **10** baby chicks, and **1** rooster live on Andi's ranch.

    How many chickens **in all** live on the ranch?
    _____ chickens live on the ranch

3. Andi's favorite hen, Miss Cluck, sat on **12** eggs. When Andi checked the next day, **8** chicks had hatched from the eggs.

    How many eggs did **NOT** hatch? _____ eggs did **NOT** hatch.

4. At breakfast, Andi ate **2** eggs, Melinda ate **1** egg, Chad ate **3** eggs, and Mitch ate **2** eggs.

    How many eggs did the family eat **in all**?

    _____ eggs   Hint: Fill in the boxes.

15

Measuring Midnight

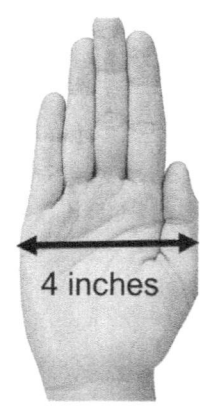

Midnight is much taller than Andi thinks. She tries three times to climb up on his back, but she falls off every time. How tall is Midnight? Horses are measured in "hands." The width of one hand is about 4 inches. Do the math. One hand = <u>4 inches</u> wide.

1. Two hands = _____ inches wide.
2. Three hands = _____ inches wide.
3. Four hands = _____ inches wide.

Now count the hands to find out how tall Midnight is.

4. Midnight is _____ hands high. He is a tall horse!

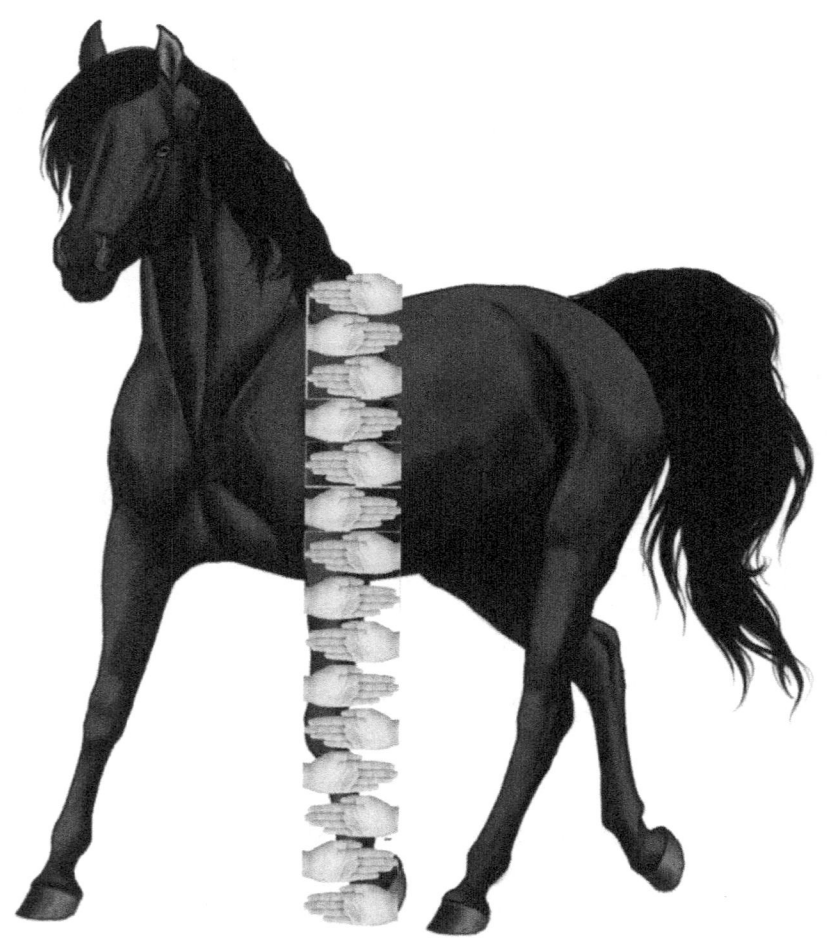

Andi's Pony Trouble Chapters 7-9

Read the chapters and answer the questions.

Chapter 7- The Best Horse

1. Midnight runs away. What does Riley do to make Midnight come back?

    A. He claps his hands.   B. He calls to Midnight.   C. He whistles.

2. Riley shows Andi a riding trick. What trick is it? _____

    _____

3. YES or NO (circle one)? Andi gallops far and fast on Midnight.

4. When it is time to go home, how does Andi get Coco to follow her?

    A. She claps her hands.   B. She calls Coco.   C. She whistles.

Chapter 8- Missing!

5. Who eats Andi's sugar cookie? _____

6. Who goes with Andi to look for Coco? Mother • Chad • nobody • Riley

7. What animal scares Andi when she is looking for Coco?

    A. a deer   B. a bear   C. a wolf   D. a mountain lion

Chapter 9- Not Big Enough

8. Andi has two great ideas for how she will get up on Midnight's back.

    Circle "yes" if her idea works. Circle "no" if her idea does not work.

    A. She climbs up on a big rock to reach Midnight's back: **YES • NO**

    B. She climbs a tree and jumped onto Midnight's back: **YES • NO**

9. YES or NO (circle one). Andi learns that she can talk to God anytime.

10. Who is all tangled up in the bushes? _____

11. Andi is (circle one) **HAPPY • SCARED • SAD** to see her pony.

New Words Chapters 7-9

Circle the meaning of each underlined word in the sentences.

1. This time Andi did not gallop. She made Midnight <u>lope</u>.

    Lope means . . .   A. a slow walk   B. faster than a trot   C. faster than a gallop

2. "I should have let go of the <u>reins</u>," Riley said.

    Reins are used to . . .   A. hold the saddle   B. catch a calf   C. guide a horse

3. Coco was <u>nibbling</u> grass.

    Nibbling means . . .   A. eating   B. stamping on   C. crushing

4. The tree branches were <u>prickly</u>.

    Prickly means . . .   A. smooth   B. scratchy   C. poison

Who Am I? Andi's Family and Friends

Who is who in Andi's family and friends? Use the clues and write their names. Color the picture.

5. I am Andi's oldest brother. _____

6. Andi calls me a "giggle box." _____

7. I was just born. I live in the barn. _____

8. Andi and I ride all over the ranch. _____

9. I am very old and a slowpoke. _____

10. I love Andi, but I tease her a lot. _____

11. I am the youngest brother. _____

12. I love all my children. _____

Help Andi Find Coco

Coco is missing! Follow the maze from Andi to Coco.

More Fun! Put together a digital puzzle of Andi, Riley, and Taffy. Go here:

CircleCBooks.com/beginnings/

Pony Trouble Chapter 10 and A Peek into the Past

Read the chapters and answer the questions.

Chapter 10- Happy Birthday, Andi!

1. Draw a picture of the cake Andi dreams about the night before her birthday. Don't forget the candles!

2. Who wakes Andi up on her birthday? _____

3. What does Andi name her brand-new foal? _____

4. What colors are Andi's new foal? Color her.

Mane: _____

Tail: _____

Body: _____

Just for fun! Watch this short video of the real-life "Taffy" (one week old) at this link:

CircleCBooks.com/beginnings/

A Peek into the Past

5. Circle the ways you could go to town in 1870 (Andi's time). Cross out the ways you could <u>not</u> go to town in 1870.

car • horse • buggy • bus • truck • wagon • van • carriage

Let's Write!

My favorite part of the story is when _____

_____

_____

_____

Andi's Sugar Cookies

Andi ate a sugar cookie when she sat on the fence with Midnight. Midnight liked the cookie as much as Andi did. Here is a recipe you can make with your parents or an older brother or sister. Cut around the dotted lines to keep it.

Andi's Sugar Cookies

Turn on the oven to 375 degrees. Wash your hands.

First you need:
2 sticks of soft butter (1 cup)
1/2 cup powdered sugar
1/2 cup white sugar

Do this:
Beat the sugar and butter together with a hand mixer.

Next:
1 egg
1/2 teaspoon vanilla
1/2 teaspoon almond extract

Add the egg, vanilla, and almond extract to the sugar and beat it well.

Last:
2 cups white flour
1/2 teaspoon baking soda
1/2 teaspoon cream of tartar

Mix in the flour, soda, and cream of tartar until the dough is firm and like a big ball.

~ Roll the dough into small balls and put them on a cookie sheet.
~ Dip the bottom of a glass in sugar and press the cookie balls down a little bit.
~ Put the cookie sheet on the top rack in the oven.
~ Set the timer for 8 minutes. The cookies are done when they are light brown around the edges. Bake a minute longer if they are not done.
~ Use a potholder to remove the cookie sheet. Cool. Enjoy! Yum!

Skinned Alive! Funny Ways to Talk

Have you ever heard someone say it's "raining cats and dogs"? Has your mom told you to "hold your horses"? Sometimes people use strange words to say something they don't really mean. These are called idioms (id-ee-ums).

Two idioms in *Pony Trouble* are:

"You are acting too big for your britches."
"I'm going to skin you alive!"

What do these idioms *really* mean? Can you figure them out?
Try it! Draw a line between each funny expression and what it really means.

1. It's raining cats and dogs.
2. That was a piece of cake!
3. You got up on the wrong side of the bed this morning.
4. Hold your horses!
5. There's something fishy going on around here.
6. I'm going to skin you alive!
7. Bite your tongue.
8. You are acting too big for your britches.

- You are grumpy this morning.
- We are having a big rainstorm.
- Slow down! Not so fast!
- That was so easy!
- Something strange is going on around here.
- You act like you know everything.
- Stop talking.
- You are in so much trouble!

Schedule for Book 2: Andi's Indian Summer

*indicates an optional activity found in the *Andi's Indian Summer* lapbook.
(Lapbook activities **can be skipped** or purchased at AndiandTaffy.com)

Indian Summer	Day 1	Day 2	Day 3	Day 4
Book	"New Words" & Chapter 1	------	Chapter 2	------
Activities	Page 25 #1-4	* Lapbook activity "New Words" & lapbook cover	Page 25 #5-9	* Lapbook activity Chapters 1-2
Indian Summer	Day 5	Day 6	Day 7	Day 8
Book	Chapter 3	------	------	Chapter 4
Activities	Page 25 #10-13	Pages 26-27	Pages 28-29	Page 30 #1-4
Indian Summer	Day 9	Day 10	Day 11	Day 12
Book	------	Chapter 5	Chapter 6	------
Activities	* Lapbook activity Chapters 3-4	Page 30 #5-7	Page 30 #8-11	* Lapbook activity Chapters 5-6
Indian Summer	Day 13	Day 14	Day 15	Day 16
Book	------	------	Chapter 7	Chapter 8
Activities	Pages 31-32	Pages 33-35	Page 37 #1-4	Page 37 #5-8
Indian Summer	Day 17	Day 18	Day 19	Day 20
Book	------	Chapter 9	------	Chapter 10
Activities	* Lapbook activity Chapters 7-8	Page 37 #9-11	Pages 38-39	Page 40 #1-4
Indian Summer	Day 21	Day 22	Day 23	Day 24
Book	------	A Peek into the Past	------	------
Activities	* Lapbook activity Chapters 9-10	Page 40 #5-6 and Let's Write!	Pages 41-43	* Lapbook activity My Favorite Part

Andi's Indian Summer Chapters 1-3

Read the chapters and answer the questions.

Chapter 1- Too Busy

1. What is Andi doing when Riley runs up to show her something?

    A. riding Coco   B. training Taffy   C. collecting eggs

2. What is the name of Taffy's mama? _____

3. YES or NO (circle one)? Andi knows how to read.

4. A dime novel costs _____ cents.

Chapter 2- Dime Novel

5. What is the name of Riley's dime novel?

   A. *The Outlaw Ranger*   B. *Pirates of the High Seas*   C. *The Indian Captive*

6. YES or NO (circle one)? Riley is a good reader.

7. Who does Riley live with on the ranch? _____

8. Where does Riley read Andi the dime novel?

     A. in the barn   B. in the tree house   C. on the porch steps

9. When Riley stops reading, what does Andi say to him?

     A. "I'm scared!"   B. "Keep reading!"   C. "I have to go eat lunch."

Chapter 3- Daydreaming

10. What is Andi daydreaming about at lunch? _____

11. Circle the brother who pulls Andi's braid. Justin • Chad • Mitch

12. What does Andi spill on her sister Melinda's lap?

     A. her soup   B. her water   C. her milk

13. YES or NO (circle one)? Andi starts getting scared of the Indian story.

New Words Chapters 1-3

Word Match- Draw a line between the words and what they mean. If you need help, look at the New Words list on page 7 in *Indian Summer*.

jim-dandy • the place in the barn where hay is kept

captive • a grassy field for horses and cows

hayloft • the men who work on a ranch

novel • very good; great

pasture • a long story; a book

cowboys • a person who is kept in a place where he or she does not want to be

More Fun with New Words

Use the words from the word box and the clues to fill in the missing words in these sentences from chapters 1-3.

1. Andi dropped Taffy's lead rope and _____. (caught her breath)

2. "Ow!" Andi _____. (yelled; shouted)

3. She picked up a kitten and _____ down in the dry, golden hay. (dropped)

4. Andi didn't know why Indians would want to _____ somebody and take them far away. (take; grab)

Word Box
hollered   gasped   capture   plopped

Dime Novels

There were no movies, TV, or the Internet in 1874, when Andi lived. Most people lived simple lives, working hard at their jobs. They stayed home the rest of the time. No one had much time to play. So, when a man named Mr. Beadle thought up the idea of dime novels, a lot of people bought them. The books told exciting stories about Indians, pirates, gold-seekers, and stagecoach robbers. Dime novels talked about strange, faraway places no one had ever heard of before. Best of all, they cost only ten cents! The stories were mostly made-up, and that's what people liked. They could pretend they were having an adventure.

Many people liked to read dime novels. President Abraham Lincoln liked them too! So many people wanted to read the stories that thousands of dime novels were published. But teachers and some parents did not like them. They did not think children should read made-up stories. They thought the books put pictures into young people's heads that should not be there. Andi found out that she should be careful what she sees and hears.

Write Your Own Dime Novel

Pretend you are living in 1874. What kind of dime novel would you like to read? On the next page, you can draw and color the cover for a story. Don't forget to write the name of your story!

My Dime Novel Cover

- Make up a title for your dime novel.
- Write your own name as the author.
- Draw a picture on the cover.
- Write your story on the next page.
- You may tell the story to your parent or older sibling, and they can write the words for you.

My Dime Novel Story

Andi's Indian Summer Chapters 4-6

Read the chapters and answer the questions.

Chapter 4- Cook

1. Who does Andi want to take with her on a ride? _____

2. What are Cook's favorite English words? _____

3. Riley would like to be an Indian boy. Circle the reasons why.

   He could sleep all day. • He could ride an Indian pony.

   He could swim in the river. • He could hunt with a bow.

4. YES or NO? Andi would like to be in Indian girl and live with the tribe.

Chapter 5- Afternoon Ride

5. What surprise does Andi get when they start riding?
   A. Taffy has grown bigger than Coco.
   B. Coco starts galloping.
   C. Snowflake runs after her.

6. YES or NO (circle one)? Taffy obeys Coco when he whinnies at her.

7. Andi thinks she and Riley are going to the meadow to ride. But Riley has a better idea. Where does he want to go? _____

Chapter 6- The Creek

8. Circle the words from the story that show Taffy is hot and tired.

   she lies down • her head hangs down • she whinnies • her tail is droopy

9. YES or NO (circle one)? Riley never finds the creek, so they go home.

10. **Who am I?** I am big, green, wet, and the biggest one Andi has ever seen! Riley found me in the creek and hid me behind his back. He gave me to Andi. I am a _____

    | Draw me. |

11. Where do the crackling noises come from?
    A. from lightning   B. from Riley stepping on a branch   C. from the bushes

New Words Chapters 4-6

Turn back to page 7 in *Indian Summer* and find the word that means a place "where the cowboys eat their meals." _____

Cook fixes food for the cowboys. Circle the food Cook might have fixed in 1874. Cross out the 4 foods that are too modern. (Hint: There were no freezers in 1874).

beef stew	ice cream sundaes	beans
pancakes	fried potatoes	doughnuts
TV dinners	scrambled eggs	biscuits
coffee	Hot Pockets	popsicles
bacon	apple pies	cornbread

More Fun with New Words

Circle the meaning of each underlined word in these sentences.

1. "I don't think I like that dime novel," Andi told Riley. "It's <u>disgusting</u>."

    Disgusting means . . .   A. scary   B. icky   C. old

2. Andi turned her back on Riley and <u>stomped</u> away.

    Stomped means . . .   A. marched loudly   B. tiptoed quietly   C. ran quickly

3. "Come back, Taffy!" Andi's heart <u>thumped</u>.

    Thumped means . . .   A. slowed down   B. stopped   C. beat fast

4. "I'm *not* little," Andi said in a <u>huff</u>.

    A huff is . . .   A. a bad mood   B. a scared gasp   C. a warning

5. "Sure I'm sure!" Riley said <u>crossly</u>.

    Crossly means . . .   A. sadly   B. happily   C. grumpily

Mystery Animal Dot-to-Dot

Who got away from Riley and Andi?

Follow the dot-to-dot puzzle from 1 to 60 to find out.

When you are finished, color the picture.

It is a _____.

Creek Animals

Andi and Riley like to play in the creek. They find a frog and have fun with it. On another day, Riley and Andi find other animals like **insects** (bugs), **fish**, **reptiles** (with scaly skin), **amphibians** (smooth skin), and **mammals** (with fur or hair). Every time they find an animal, Riley writes it down.

Can you help put the animals they saw at the creek into their special animal groups? (on this page and the next page). You can also draw a picture if you know what the animal looks like. When you are finished, cut out the pages and staple them together to create a book. Color the cover "Creek Animals."

Use these animals to write in your "Creek Animals" book.

trout	frog	turtle	fox	beaver
bobcat	salamander	snake	minnow	fly
water bug	dragonfly	mosquito	bee	deer

More Creek Animals

REPTILES

AMPHIBIANS

MAMMALS

FISH

Andi's Indian Summer Chapters 7-9

Read the chapters and answer the questions.

Chapter 7- Snapping and Crackling

1. Riley thinks the snapping and crackling noises in the bushes come from . . .

    A. a rabbit   B. a beaver   C. a skunk   D. all of these

2. Who does Andi think is making the snapping noise? _____

3. Who is right (circle one)?   **ANDI** • **RILEY**

4. Which horse does the tall Indian boy take? _____

Chapter 8- Too Many Indians!

5. YES or NO. When they see the Indians, both Andi and Riley start to cry.

6. This Indian tribe has a name. It starts with a "Y." _____

7. What is the grown-up Indian's name? _____

8. Why can't the grown-up Indian man take Andi and Riley home?

    A. He doesn't know where the Circle C ranch is.

    B. He doesn't want to leave his people.

    C. It is too late in the day to go so far.

Chapter 9- Yokut Camp

9. Andi and Riley must do something they do not want to do. What is it?

    A. Andi and Riley must give the Indians their horses.

    B. Andi and Riley must spend the night with the Indians.

    C. Andi and Riley must walk home in the dark.

10. Circle the things Andi sees in the beautiful Yokut baskets.

    pine cones • beads • acorns • pebbles • berries • shells

11. The Yokut Indians use hot _____ to heat their acorn mush.

Word Puzzle Chapters 7-9

Use the clues to fill in the missing letters of the words in this puzzle. Then watch the Yokut Indians make acorn mush at:
CircleCBooks.com/beginnings/

Y __ __ __ __ __   Riley did this when the Indian boy took Midnight. Another word for "shouted."

O __ __ __   This word means "no" in Yokut.

K __ __ __   The Yokuts were very _____ to Andi and Riley. They took care of them.

U __ __ __ __   Sid, the ranch boss, is Riley's _____.

T __ __ __ __   This is the name of Andi's foal.

✳ ✳ ✳ ✳

I __ __ __ __ __   This word means the opposite of <u>outside</u>.

N __ __ __ __   Riley read Andi a dime _____.

D __ __   This word means the opposite of <u>night</u>.

I __ __   Frozen water is called _____.

A __ __ __ __ __ __   The mush Andi and Riley ate with the Yokuts was made from _____.

N __ __ __   Acorns, pecans, almonds, and walnuts are different kinds of _____.

S __ __ __ __ __ __   The four seasons are spring, _____, fall, and winter.

Yokut Baskets

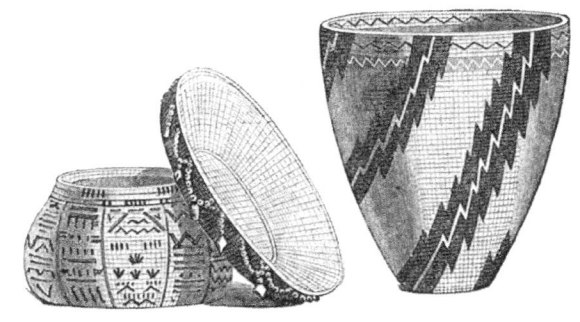

The Yokuts made beautiful baskets from the reeds that grew next to the rivers and lakes. They wove pretty designs in the baskets, which came in all sizes and shapes.

Yokut baskets were woven so tightly that they could hold water without leaking. But they could not put the baskets over the fire, or they would burn up. Instead, the Yokut women heated rocks in the fire. They used sticks to drop the hot rocks into baskets of water, deer stew, or acorn mush. The Yokuts made other baskets for baby cradles, for storing acorns and other items, and for playing games.

Weave a Placemat

You can make a placemat using the same type of weaving the Yokuts used.

You will need:
- one piece of colored construction paper for the background
- colored paper for the strips
- scissors and a glue stick

Follow these steps:

1. Choose one color for the background and fold it in half.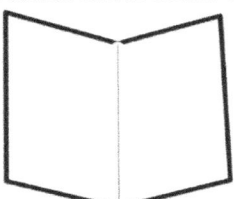

2. Cut slices in the paper so it looks like this: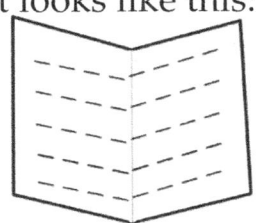

3. Cut narrow (one-inch) strips from the other colors.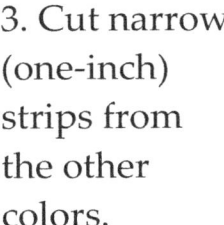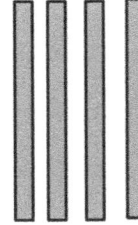

4. Weave the colored strips in and out of the background paper.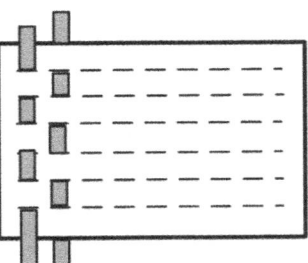

5. Trim the ends of the strips (if needed) and glue them down.

Indian Summer Chapter 10 and a Peek into the Past

Read the chapters and answer the questions.

Chapter 10- Good-bye

1. What is the name of Andi's new friend? _____

2. Draw the gift Andi's new friend gives her. ⟶

3. Draw the gift Andi gives her new friend.

    What color is this gift? _____

4. Draw and color the gift Chad gives Lum-pa.

A Peek into the Past

5. Circle the kinds of jobs children did in 1874.

    worked in factories • fixed watches and clocks

    fixed bicycles • picked crops (fruits and veggies)

    took care of cows and sheep

6. YES or NO (circle one)? Many teachers and parents did not want children to read dime novels.

Let's Write!

Circle a character from *Indian Summer*. Write two sentences about that character. Start each sentence with a capital letter. Use a period at the end.

Andi • Riley • Lum-pa • Ku-yu • Choo-nook • Cook • Taffy • Midnight

_____

_____

_____

_____

Alike and Different

Andi and her new friend Choo-nook are very different from each other. However, they are alike in some ways too. Cut out the words below. Paste the words that describe Andi in the "Andi" circle. Paste the words that describe Choo-nook in the "Choo-nook" circle. Paste the words that describe both girls (how they are alike) in the middle, where the circles meet.

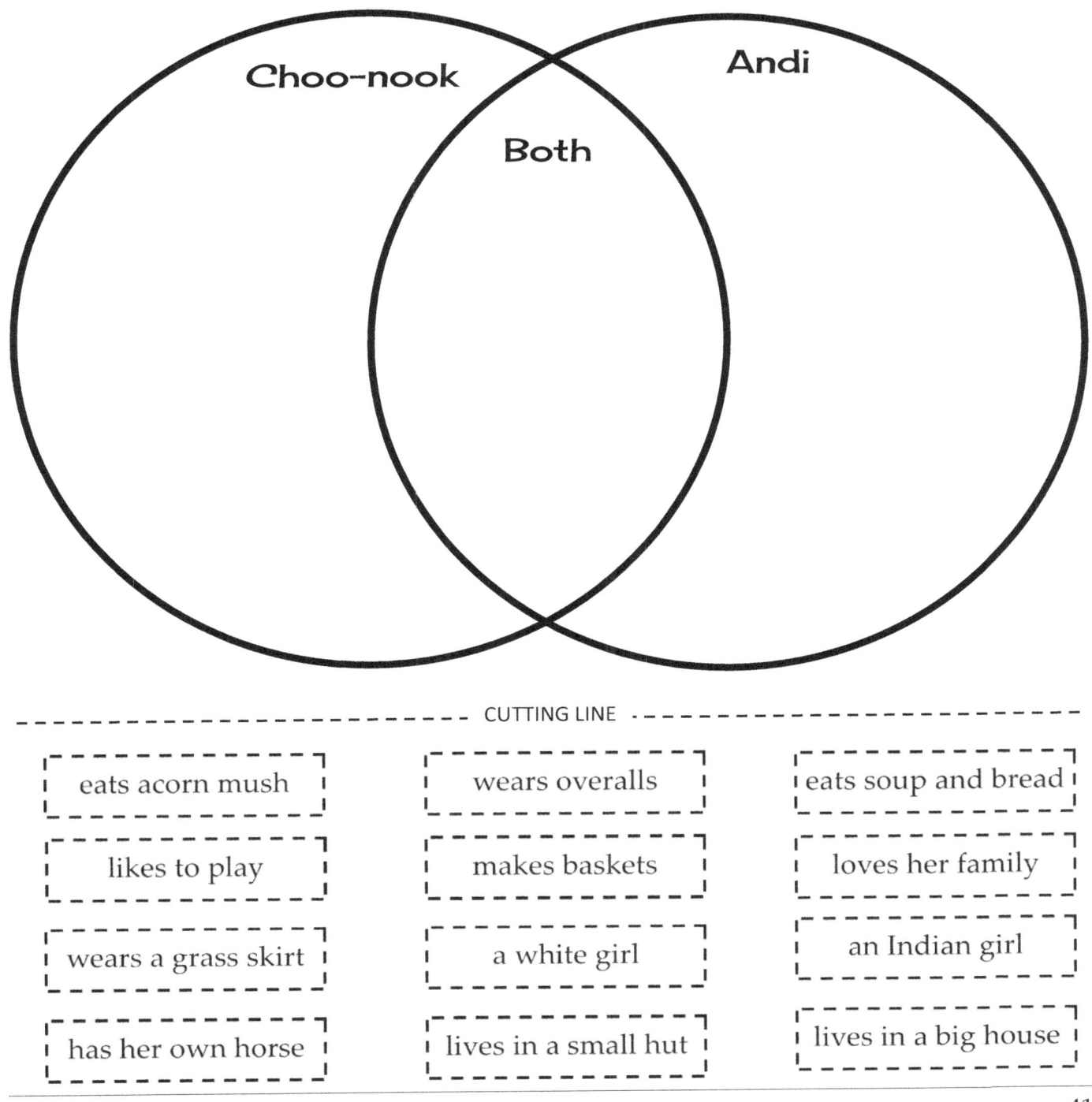

- CUTTING LINE -

eats acorn mush	wears overalls	eats soup and bread
likes to play	makes baskets	loves her family
wears a grass skirt	a white girl	an Indian girl
has her own horse	lives in a small hut	lives in a big house

41

Character Trait – Diligence
Doing my best to complete a task without giving up.

Whatever you do, work at it with all your heart.
Colossians 3:23

Diligence

God wants us to do our best in everything we do. Andi must be diligent when she trains Taffy, or her foal will grow up to be wild and untamed.

What does it mean to be <u>diligent</u> for the Lord? Work the puzzle to find out.

ACROSS:
2. Diligent people <u>WORK</u> hard.
4. They always _____ their best.
5. They _____ what they start and do not give up.
6. They do not _____ about a hard or messy job.
8. Diligent people are not _____.

DOWN:
1. Diligent people are _____ for what God does for them.
3. They _____ God to help them when things get hard.
7. They _____ quickly.

WORD BOX
OBEY
~~WORK~~
LAZY
FINISH
TRY
TRUST
GRATEFUL
COMPLAIN

43

Schedule for Book 3: **Andi's Fair Surprise**

*indicates an optional activity found in the *Andi's Fair Surprise* lapbook.
(Lapbook activities **can be skipped** or purchased at AndiandTaffy.com)

Fair Surprise	**Day 1**	**Day 2**	**Day 3**	**Day 4**
Book	"New Words" & Chapter 1	Chapter 2	———	———
Activities	Page 45 #1-3	Page 45 #4-7	* Lapbook activity Chapters 1-2 (#1) & Lapbook cover	* Lapbook activity Chapters 1-2 (#2)
Fair Surprise	**Day 5**	**Day 6**	**Day 7**	**Day 8**
Book	Chapter 3	———	———	Chapter 4
Activities	Page 45 #8-11	Pages 46-47	Pages 48-49	Page 50 #1-4
Fair Surprise	**Day 9**	**Day 10**	**Day 11**	**Day 12**
Book	———	Chapter 5	Chapter 6	———
Activities	* Lapbook activity Chapters 3-4	Page 50 #5-8	Page 50 #9-13	* Lapbook activity Chapters 5-6
Fair Surprise	**Day 13**	**Day 14**	**Day 15**	**Day 16**
Book	———	———	Chapter 7	Chapter 8
Activities	Pages 51-52	Page 53	Page 54 #1-5	Page 55 #6-9
Fair Surprise	**Day 17**	**Day 18**	**Day 19**	**Day 20**
Book	———	———	Chapter 9	———
Activities	* Lapbook activity Chapters 7-8 (#1)	* Lapbook activity Chapters 7-8 (#2)	Page 54 #10-13	Page 55-56
Fair Surprise	**Day 21**	**Day 22**	**Day 23**	**Day 24**
Book	Chapter 10	A Peek into the Past	———	———
Activities	Page 57 #1-4	Page 57 #5-7 and Let's Write!	Pages 58-61	* Lapbook activity Chapters 9-10

Andi's Fair Surprise Chapters 1-3

Read the chapters and answer the questions.

Chapter 1- Ribbons and Roosters

1. What is the name of Andi's dog? _____

2. Where is Henry the rooster in this chapter?

    A. in a cage   B. in the barn   C. in the henhouse

3. YES or NO (circle one)? Andi gets to take Taffy to the fair!

Chapter 2- All Tied Up

4. Andi has three big brothers. Circle the brother who lassoed her:

    Justin   •   Chad   •   Mitch

5. Draw a line from the person to what he or she is taking to the fair:

Mother	lots of cows and horses
Chad & Mitch	nothing
Melinda	jars of jelly
Riley	a quilt
Andi	Henry the rooster

6. Who must Andi apologize to for acting up? _____

7. YES or NO (circle one)? Andi is very excited to dress up for the fair.

Chapter 3- The Black Beast

8. Who sits next to Andi on the train? _____

9. Circle the things that happen to Andi when the train starts going fast.

    she falls asleep • she bumps her nose • she cries

    she falls on the floor • her hat slips down • her stomach feels sick

10. What blows into the train when Andi opens the window? _____

11. (Circle one): <u>Riley</u> • <u>Justin</u> explains to Andi how a steam train works.

New Words Chapters 1-3

Word Match- Draw a line between the words and what they mean. If you need help, look at the New Words list on page 7 in *Fair Surprise*.

calf • not exciting; boring

dull • a baby cow

foreman • someone who helps the rancher take care of the ranch

lasso • tiny specks of leftover wood or coal after it is burned

soot • a rope with a loop tied at one end

More Fun with New Words

Use the words from the word box and the clues to fill in the missing words in these sentences from chapters 1-3.

1. Bossy old Chad. He was always _____ her great ideas. (ruining; messing up)

2. Chad was always _____ Andi. (kidding; pestering)

3. Chad _____ Andi's hair and stood up. (messed up; rumpled)

4. Andi smiled. She liked sitting by Justin. He was always _____. (understanding)

5. The train went faster. It _____ back and forth. (rocked)

Word Box
teasing   patient   spoiling   swayed   ruffled

Where Is the State Fair?

Sacramento is the capital of California. The state fair has been held there every year, starting in 1859. Andi and her family live in Fresno. It is a long way from Andi's ranch to the state fair. It takes many hours on the train to get there.

This is a map of California. Do these things:

1. Draw and color a red star ☆ on the dot under the word "Sacramento" to show it is the capital of California.
2. Write "Fresno" on the line next to the large dot to show where Andi lives.
3. Draw railroad tracks ┼┼┼┼ from the dot at Fresno to the star at Sacramento, to show the train trip Andi took to the State Fair.

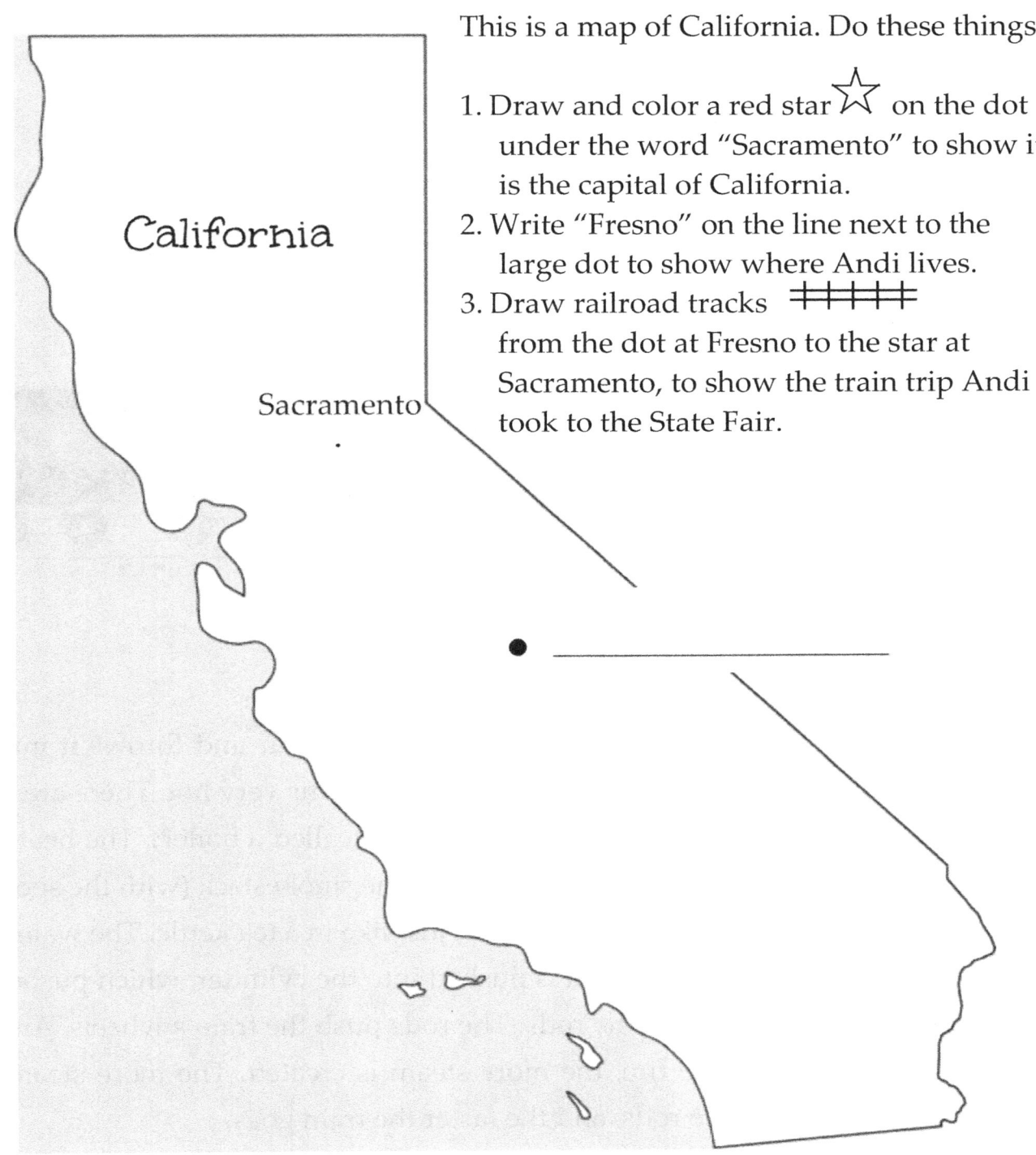

Steam Trains

"The engine burns coal, and that makes the train go," Riley explains to Andi. "The more coal it burns, the faster it goes. The leftover coal goes out the smokestack."

* * *

How does burning coal make a train go? What else happens? Here is a train engine and its coal car. To make it go, the train needs:

1. coal
2. a firebox
3. water
4. a water tank (boiler)
5. cylinders & pistons
6. rods to push the wheels
7. a smokestack

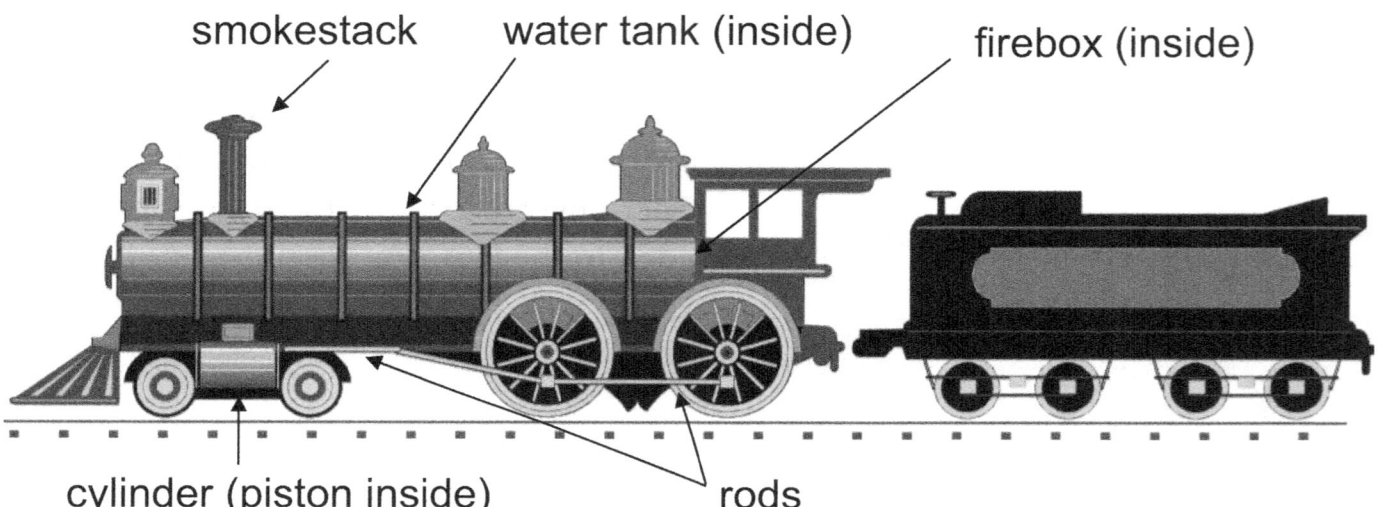

Here's what happens:

The fireman takes big shovelfuls of coal from the coal car and throws it into the firebox, which sits inside the train engine. The coal burns very hot. There are pipes running from the firebox through a big water tank (called a boiler). The heat from the burning coal goes through the pipes and out the smokestack (with the soot). As it goes through the pipes, the water heats up, just like in a tea kettle. The water gets so hot it turns into steam. The steam is pushed into the cylinder, which pushes the piston. Then the piston pushes the rods. The rods push the train's wheels. And the train moves! The hotter the fire, the more steam is created. The more steam, the faster the piston pushes the rods, and the faster the train goes.

Inside a Steam Engine

Follow a piece of coal step by step as it turns into steam and makes the train's wheels go around. Color carefully! Watch how a steam train works at this link:

CircleCBooks.com/beginnings/

1. COAL: The train burns coal inside the firebox.
2. FIREBOX: Color the firebox **RED** for a HOT fire!
3. HEATING TUBES: The heat, smoke, and coal dust go through these tubes. Color the heating tubes **RED**. They are HOT.
4. WATER TANK (BOILER): the tubes run through the boiler and heat up the water. Color the water in the boiler **BLUE**.
5. SMOKESTACK: the smoke and soot (burned coal) go up the smokestack. Draw **BLACK** smoke going up the smokestack.
6. STEAM: The water in the boiler gets so hot it turns into steam and goes up. Color everything here **GRAY**, like hot steam.
7. CYLINDER: The steam goes into the cylinder. Color the cylinder **GRAY**. It is full of steam too.
8. PISTON: The steam pushes the piston. Color the piston **PURPLE**.
9. RODS: The piston pushes the rods. Color the rods **GREEN**.
10. WHEELS: Rods push and pull the train's wheels. Color the wheels **BROWN**.
11. SMOKESTACK: The piston pushes the steam back through a little door. It goes up the smokestack too. Color this part of the smokestack **GRAY**

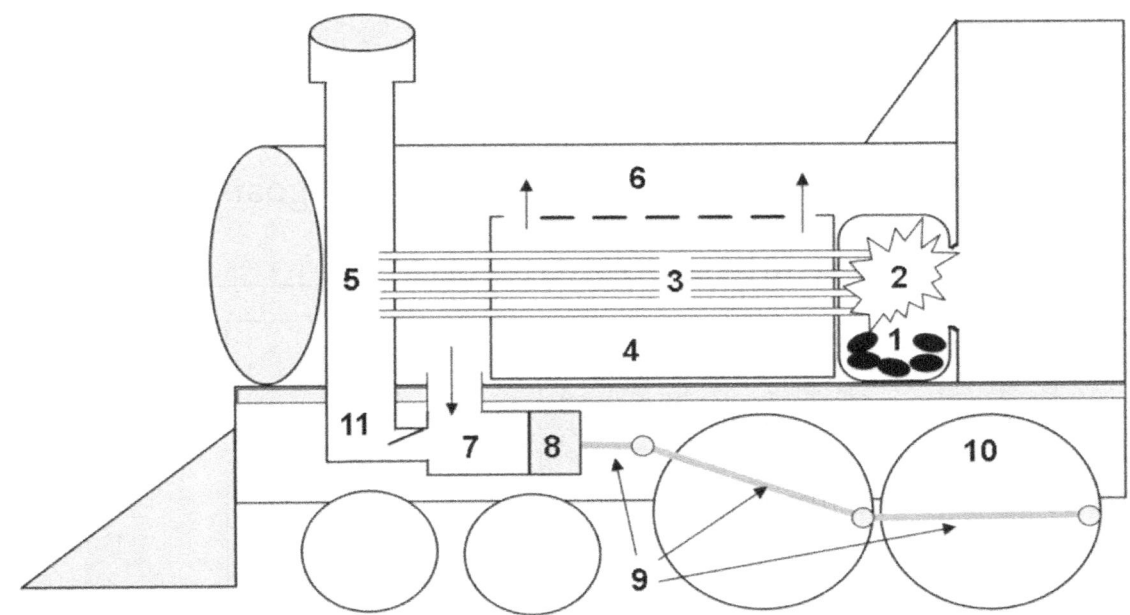

Andi's Fair Surprise Chapters 4-6

Read the chapters and answer the questions.

Chapter 4- Surprises

1. Andi falls asleep on the train and wakes up in a _____

2. The fair lasts (circle one):   3 days   •   5 days   •   one week

3. Andi forgets her _____ in the dining room and runs back for it.

4. What does Andi find on the table next to her hat?

   A. two shiny dimes   B. a nickel and five pennies   C. a hair bow

Chapter 5- Tickets

5. The state fair is held in which city?

   A. San Francisco   B. Sacramento   C. San Diego

6. Andi's fair ticket is number _____

7. Where does Andi keep her fair ticket so it stays safe?

   A. in Justin's pocket   B. with Mother   C. pinned inside her pocket

8. YES or NO (circle one). Justin gives Andi 20 cents to spend at the fair.

Chapter 6- Fair Day

9. Circle the animals Riley and Andi visit on their first day at the fair.

   cats • rabbits • horses • sheep • chickens • cows • goats • dogs • pigs

10. What is the name of the little girl Andi meets? _____

11. Draw Andi's first-favorite animal.

12. Draw Andi's second-favorite animal.

13. What is your favorite animal?

   _____

First-favorite animal	Second-favorite animal

New Words Chapters 4-6

Turn back to page 7 in *Fair Surprise* and find the three words below. Write what each word means.

1. **exhibits** _____

   _____

2. **livestock** _____

3. **thrill show** _____

New Words Riddles

Can you guess the word from the riddle clues? Use the word box for help.

4. You look at me in a restaurant to decide what you would like to eat and how much it will cost. What am I? _____

5. You need me to get into the fair or a movie theater, or to ride a plane. What am I? _____

6. I am a lady who writes down what you want to eat when you go to a restaurant. Who am I? _____

7. When someone spins me around, I turn wool into yarn. What am I? _____

   spinning wheel

8. People give this to someone who has done an extra-good job serving another person. What am I? _____

Word Box
spinning wheel   waitress   menu   ticket   tip

Fair Math

Andi and Riley count the animals they see at the fair. They use tally marks like this to keep track of the animals: |||

Count the tally marks (count by 5's) to find out how many of each kind of animal Andi and Riley saw at the fair.

Horses: |||| |||| |||| |||| |||| |||| || _____

Cows: |||| |||| |||| |||| |||| ||| _____

Pigs: |||| |||| |||| |||| _____

Chickens: |||| |||| |||| |||| |||| |||| |||| | _____

Sheep: |||| |||| |||| |||| |||| _____

1. Which animal did Andi and Riley see the most of? _____

2. Which animal did Andi and Riley see the least of? _____

3. How many different *kinds* of animals did Andi and Riley see? _____

Which is your favorite fair animal? Circle your choice below:

Who Am I?

Today at the fair you can see many different kinds of animals. You can even bring your pets and win ribbons.

Below are some clues about some of the animals at the fair. Can you guess which animal it is? Use the word box to help you.

```
cat     turkey    rabbit    duck     goat      dog
cow     sheep     pig       hen      rooster   horse
```

1. I have beautiful tail feathers, and I crow every morning. _____

2. Children love to pet my soft fur. I have long ears and hop. _____

3. I don't mean to, but I smell stinky. I grunt and like the mud. _____

4. Most of the time you see me at Thanksgiving, on a table. _____

5. Fluffy wool covers me all winter. I get it cut off in the spring. _____

6. I like to butt heads, and sometimes I have horns. _____

7. Children like to ride me. I am Andi's favorite animal. _____

8. I lay an egg every morning. Andi has to collect my eggs. _____

9. Swimming is what I like to do! I can fly too, and quack. _____

10. I give a lot of milk every day. My baby is called a "calf." _____

11. I make a fine pet. I love to run and play. I bark a lot. _____

12. I don't like dogs! I am soft and cuddly and like to purr: _____

13. Which of the animals from the word box do you like best? _____

Andi's Fair Surprise Chapters 7-9

Read the chapters and answer the questions.

Chapter 7- The Prize

1. YES or NO (circle one)? Mitch wins the horse race at the fair.

2. The strong man lifts a _____ to his shoulders.

3. How much money does Justin give Andi every day to spend? _____

4. What does Andi find that she likes better than a thrill show or taffy candy?

    A. a pony ride   B. a ring-toss game   C. looking at exhibits

5. What prize does Andi want to win? _____

Chapter 8- Winning Ticket

6. Why does Andi cry on the last day of the fair?

    A. She wants to stay.   B. She fell down.   C. She didn't win the hat.

7. Henry the rooster wins (circle one) **FIRST** • **SECOND** • **THIRD** place.

8. What does Andi win with her fair ticket?

    A. a lamb   B. the cowboy hat with a red feather   C. taffy candy

9. Circle the people who do NOT like sheep:

  Andi • Uncle Sid • Chad • Jesus • Carrie • other ranchers

Chapter 9- Lamb Trouble

10. What name does Andi give her new lamb? _____

11. YES or NO (circle one)? Andi's lamb makes a mess of the fair.

12. Who picks up the lamb (circle one)? Melinda • Riley • Andi • Chad

13. Who does Riley see coming toward them?

    _____ and _____

Twenty Cents a Day

Justin gives Andi 20 cents each day of the fair. She can spend it on anything she wants. Below are some of the things Andi buys. Can you help her add it up?

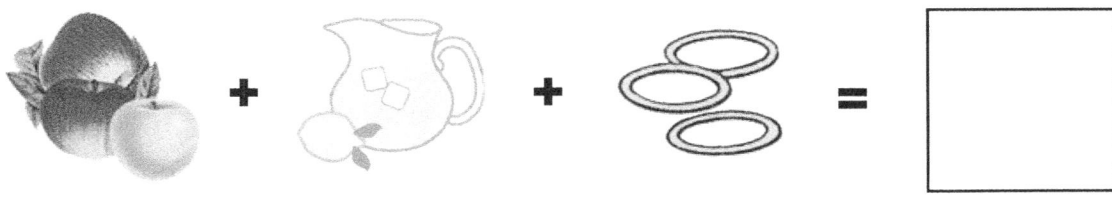

```
Price List
Fruit = 7 cents        Bread & Jam = 6 cents     Ring Toss Game = 5 cents
Thrill Show = 5 cents  Lemonade = 4 cents        Taffy Candy = 3 cents
```

Fruit + Lemonade + Ring Toss = ☐

Lemonade + Bread & Jam + Fruit + Ring Toss = ☐

Ring Toss + Ring Toss + Thrill Show = ☐

Ring Toss + Ring Toss + Ring Toss + Ring Toss = ☐

What did Andi spend most of her money on? _____

Third Place Winner

Follow the dot-to-dot to find out who wins a third-place ribbon at the state fair. Who is it? _____ Why doesn't he win a first-place blue ribbon? (Look on page 55 of *Fair Surprise* for a hint.)

_____

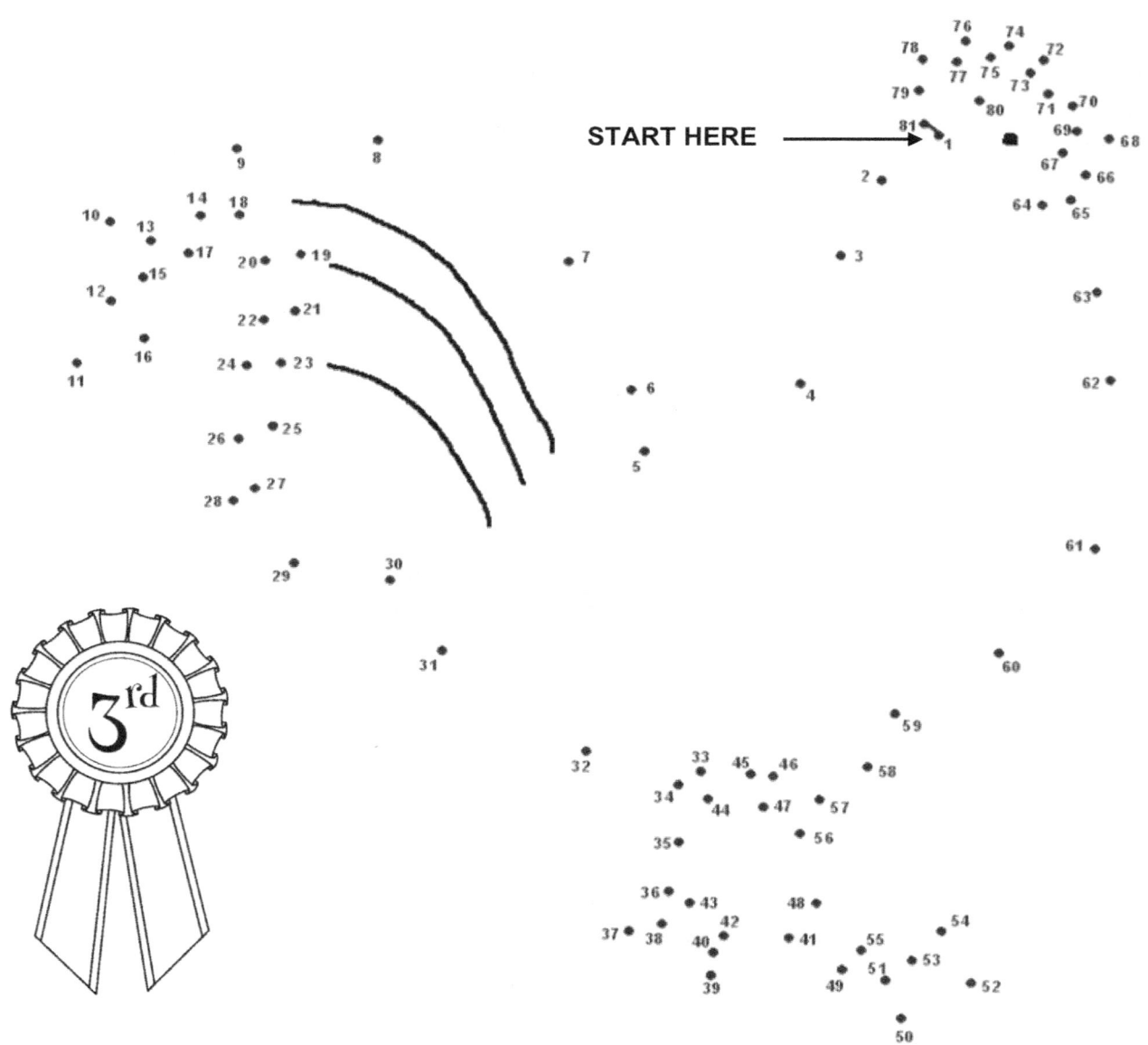

Now color the picture. Make this fellow beautiful! Color the ribbon too.

56

Fair Surprise Chapter 10 and A Peek into the Past

Read the chapters and answer the questions.

Chapter 10- Blue Ribbon

1. Andi gives the lamb to (circle one): Melinda • Mother • Carrie

2. Why is Andi sad after she gives Inky away?

    A. She has a stomach ache from too much fair food.

    B. The fair is over, and she doesn't want to leave.

    C. She doesn't have anything to take home from the fair.

3. What does Chad win for Andi? _____

4. What does Mother give Andi when the fair is over?

    A. a blue ribbon   B. a big hug   C. prize money

A Peek into the Past

5. In what year did the California State Fair begin? _____

6. YES or NO (circle one)? There were lots of rides at the fair, even at first.

7. Name three things you might see at the fair.

    _____   _____   _____

Let's Write!

What was your favorite part of *Andi's Fair Surprise* and why? Write two sentences. Use periods at the end of your sentences.

My favorite part of this story was when _____

_____

_____

Character Ribbons

Part of the fun of a state fair is entering something special with the hope of winning a ribbon (and prize money). People like to win ribbons for the best horse, the biggest pumpkin, the tastiest pie, or the most beautiful quilt. A blue ribbon means you won first place; a red ribbon means second place; and a white ribbon means third place.

Andi wanted to win a blue ribbon by taking Taffy to the fair. Instead, she won a blue ribbon from her mother for making a hard choice.

She won a "character ribbon." Character is something on the inside of a person, like being grateful or patient or truthful or obedient. Andi won her character ribbon for being KIND and BRAVE. She gave up her lamb.

On the next page are character ribbon bookmarks for you to color and cut out (you can make more copies of the page). Think of something your mother, father, sister, or brother could win a character ribbon for. Write it in the middle of the ribbon. Color and decorate the ribbon (you can add glitter too). Cut out the bookmark and give it to them.

Now ask your parents what YOU could win a character ribbon for. Write their answer in the middle of a ribbon. Color and decorate a character ribbon for yourself. Cut it out and keep it handy. Use these character ribbons as bookmarks or to hang on your wall.

You can also use the sample character circles for your character ribbon bookmarks.

Character Ribbon Bookmarks

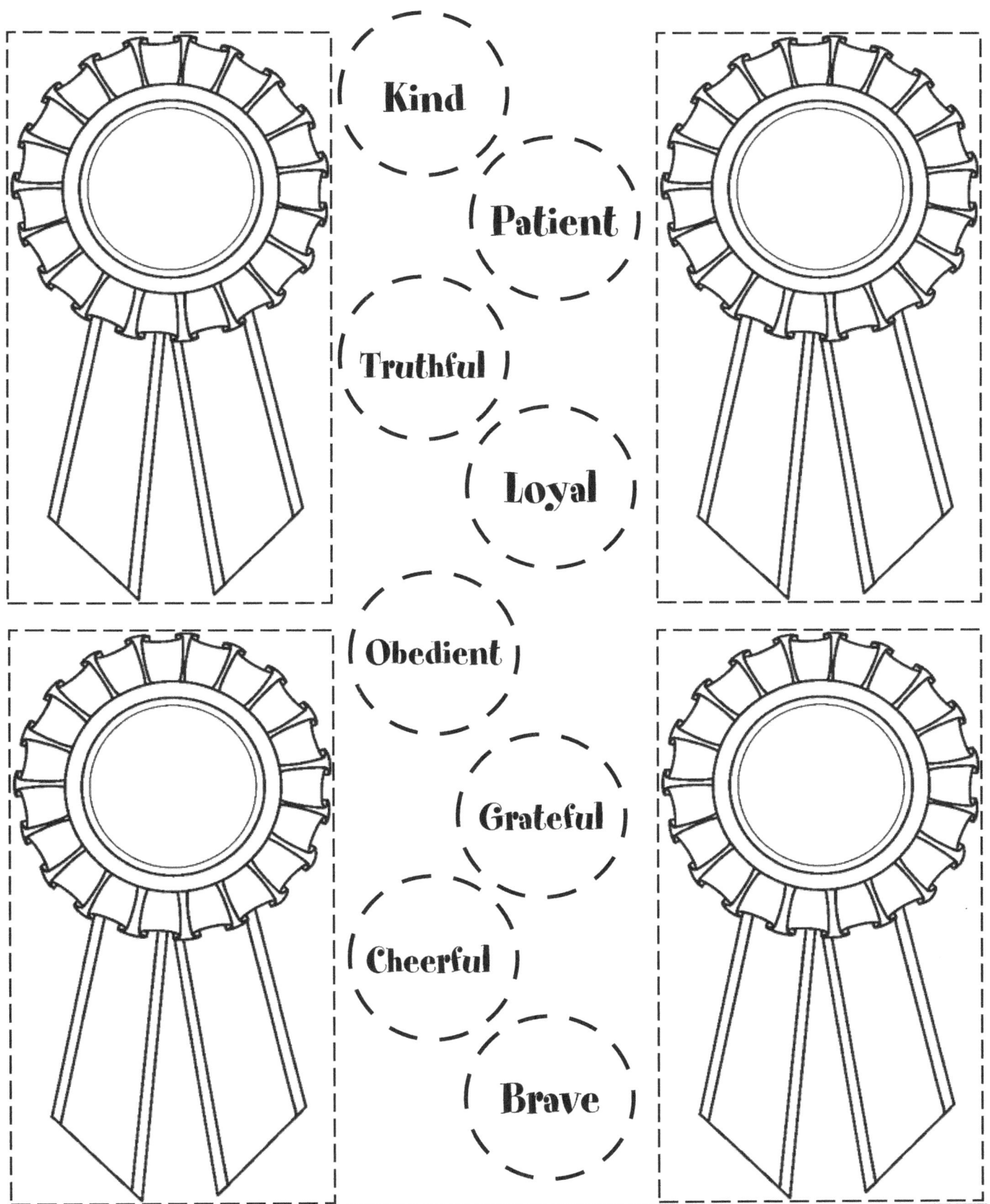

59

Character Trait - Security
Building my life around what cannot be taken away.

When you are secure, you feel safe. God loves you. No matter what happens, you can trust Him to take care of you in this life . . . and forever.

Fill in the missing words from the Bible verses to show God's promises to keep you secure in Him. (Use your Bible to find the verses or use the word box.)

1. (Romans 8:28) For _____ causes all things to work together for _____ to those that love God.

2. (Romans 8:39) [Nothing] can separate us from the _____ of God.

3. (Psalm 23:1) The LORD is my _____

4. (Psalm 23:4) Even though I walk through the darkest _____ I will fear no _____, for you are with me.

5. (Psalm 48:14) For this God is our God _____ and ever.

6. (Psalm 100:3) We are his _____ and the sheep of his _____.

Schedule for Book 4: Andi's Scary School Days

*indicates an optional activity found in the *Andi's Scary School Days* lapbook.
(Lapbook activities **can be skipped** or purchased at AndiandTaffy.com)

Scary School Days	Day 1	Day 2	Day 3	Day 4
Book	"New Words" & Chapter 1	Chapter 2	———	Chapter 3
Activities	Page 63 #1-5	Page 63 #6-8	*Lapbook activity Chapters 1-2 & Lapbook cover*	Page 63 #9-11
Scary School Days	**Day 5**	**Day 6**	**Day 7**	**Day 8**
Book	———	———	Chapter 4	———
Activities	Pages 64-65	Pages 66-67	Page 68 #1-4	*Lapbook activity Chapters 3-4*
Scary School Days	**Day 9**	**Day 10**	**Day 11**	**Day 12**
Book	Chapter 5	Chapter 6	———	———
Activities	Page 68 #5-8	Page 68 #9-14	*Lapbook activity Chapters 5-6*	Pages 69-70
Scary School Days	**Day 13**	**Day 14**	**Day 15**	**Day 16**
Book	———	Chapter 7	Chapter 8	———
Activities	Pages 71-75	Page 77 #1-4	Page 77 #5-7	*Lapbook activity Chapters 7-8 (#1)*
Scary School Days	**Day 17**	**Day 18**	**Day 19**	**Day 20**
Book	———	Chapter 9	———	Chapter 10
Activities	*Lapbook activity Chapters 7-8 (#2)*	Page 77 #8-11	Pages 78-79	Page 80 #1-3
Scary School Days	**Day 21**	**Day 22**	**Day 23**	**Day 24**
Book	———	A Peek into the Past	———	———
Activities	*Lapbook activity Chapters 9-10*	Page 80 #4-7 and Let's Write!	Pages 81-83	*Lapbook activity 5 story elements*

Andi's Scary School Days Chapters 1-3

Read the chapters and answer the questions.

Chapter 1- Hide and Seek

1. <u>Where</u> is Andi hiding when the story begins? _____

2. <u>Why</u> is Andi hiding?

    A. She's playing hide-and-seek with Riley

    B. She doesn't want to go to school.

    C. She's in trouble again.

3. Who finds Andi first (circle one)?   Mother • Justin • Chad • Riley

4. Who finds Andi second (circle one)?   Mother • Justin • Chad • Riley

5. Big sister Melinda thinks Andi looks like . . .

    A. a tomboy   B. a wild Indian   C. a little lady

Chapter 2- China Doll or Tomboy?

6. Andi has 3 big brothers. Which brother gave her a rattlesnake's rattle?

    Justin   •   Chad   •   Mitch

7. YES or NO (circle one)? Melinda is excited to start a new school year.

8. How does Melinda know it is time to go inside?

    A. The teacher calls the pupils.

    B. A boy rings the school bell.

    C. The children run up the steps.

Chapter 3- Miss Hall

9. YES or NO (circle one)? Andi already knows all the letters of the alphabet.

10. "Andi" is a nickname. What is Andi's real name? _____

11. Cory, the little boy sitting next to Andi, throws something at her. What?

    A. a spider   B. a lizard   C. a dead fly

New Words Chapters 1-3

Word Match- Draw a line between the words and what they mean. If you need help, look at the New Words list on page 7 in *Scary School Days*.

tomboy • the dried, pale-yellow stems left over from wheat or oats

scaredy-cat • a ruffled apron worn over a dress

straw • a girl who likes to dress and play like a boy

pinafore • someone who is afraid

blackboard • a large, smooth dark surface for writing on with chalk

More Fun with New Words

Use the words from the word box and the clues to fill in the missing words in these sentences from chapters 1-3.

1. "Put me down!" Andi hollered. She _____ to get free. (wiggled; twisted)

2. "Tell her not to make a _____," Melinda begged. (argument)

3. "Your little sister is _____," Sarah said. (cute; sweet)

4. When Aunt Rebecca came for a visit, she always _____ Andi. (got after; corrected)

5. The fly was a _____ black dot. (crushed; squashed)

Word Box
adorable   squirmed   scolded   fuss   squished

The United States Flag in 1874

This is the flag Andi saw in her schoolroom in 1874. If you look closely, you will see it is a little different from our flag today.

Answer the questions.

1. Count the stars on this 1874 flag. How many stars are there? _____
2. The stars stand for the number of states in our country. How many states were there in the United States in 1874? _____
3. Count the stripes. How many stripes are there? _____
4. The stripes stand for the number of original American colonies there were at first. How many colonies were there? _____
5. Count the stars in our flag below. How many stars are there today? _____
6. How many states are in the United States today? _____
7. How many stripes are in our flag today? _____
8. Color our flag.

Andi's Schoolroom

Andi goes to school in a one-room schoolhouse. Here is a map of Andi's classroom. Use the map key to find your way around:

1. Find the flag in the schoolroom and color it red.

2. Andi sits in the desk next to the flag. She also sits across the aisle from Cory. Write an "A" on Andi's desk and a "C" on Cory's desk.

3. Color the blackboard black.

4. Draw a fire inside the wood stove.

5. Put an "X" on the teacher's desk.

6. Cory likes to stand in the corner, so he can look out the window. Which corner do you think that is? Draw Cory standing in the corner.

7. Melinda sits behind Andi, in the 4th row. Write an "M" on Melinda's desk.

8. How many pupils' seats does Andi's classroom hold? (count by 2's) _____

Map Key

- flag
- teacher's desk
- blackboard
- wood stove
- pupils' desk
- globe
- door
- windows

The Song "America"

One of the songs children sang in school was "America." A man by the name of Reverend Samuel F. Smith wrote the song in 1832. You might know the song by another name: "My Country, 'Tis of Thee."

Listen to "America" by going to this link:

CircleCBooks.com/beginnings/

Below is the first verse of "America." Read the song. Do you know what all the words mean?

"America"
My country, 'tis of <u>thee</u>,
Sweet land of <u>liberty</u>,
Of <u>thee</u> I sing;
Land where my fathers died,
Land of the <u>Pilgrims</u>' <u>pride</u>,
From every mountain side
Let freedom ring.

Four words in the song are <u>underlined</u>. These are words you might not know. Draw a line to match the word with what you think it means.

thee • freedom

liberty • a very old-fashioned word that means "you"

Pilgrims • when you feel good inside about doing something well

pride • the people who came to America aboard the *Mayflower*

Andi's Scary School Days Chapters 4-6

Read the chapters and answer the questions.

Chapter 4- Too Many Rules!

1. What 4 words did Riley teach Andi before she went to school?

   _____ _____ _____ _____ _____

2. YES or NO (circle one)? Andi knows how to jump rope.

3. What does Andi do when she gets upset about the jump rope?
   A. She runs back into the classroom. B. She cries. C. She climbs a tree.

4. Who tells Andi to come down out of the tree? _____

Chapter 5- Tree Trouble

5. YES or NO (circle one)? Melinda climbs up and gets Andi out of the tree.

6. Melinda tells Miss Hall that Andi is not afraid of anything. But that is not exactly true. What is Andi afraid of? _____

7. Andi is in trouble because (circle one) A. she doesn't obey the teacher
       B. she talks back to Justin   C. she falls out of the tree

8. What falls out of Andi's pocket? _____

Chapter 6- Tardy Means Late

9. Who does not go to school the next morning? _____

10. What does "tardy" mean? _____

11. What color is the belly of Cory's lizard? _____

12. What is the name of Cory's lizard? _____

13. YES or NO (circle one)? Andi is afraid of lizards and other creatures.

14. What falls into the teacher's lap?   an apple • the lizard • a bottle of ink

68

New Words Chapters 4-6

Word Match- Draw a line between the words and what they mean. If you need help, look at the New Words list on page 7 in *Scary School Days*.

ma'am • a small blackboard each pupil uses to write their lessons with chalk

pupil • like "Mrs."; a polite way to talk to a lady

slate • late

tardy • a pupil in school

New Words Riddles

Can you guess the words from the riddle clues? Use the word box for help.

1. This is what the teacher gives a pupil who does not obey the school rules. What am I? _____

2. Andi thinks I am only used to lasso a calf or a horse. But I can be used for a fun game too. What am I? _____

3. Judges and lawyers work here. What am I? _____

4. A branch did this to Andi's pinafore and tore her pocket open.

_____

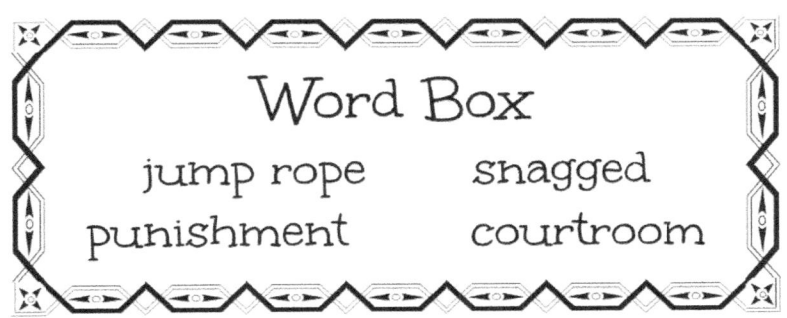

Word Box

jump rope   snagged
punishment   courtroom

Copy Work

Children in the 1800s did a lot of copy work. Teachers expected their pupils to have nice writing. Why? There were no typewriters or computers in the 1800s. Most things were written by hand, and people needed to be able to read what you wrote. It was also a sign of a well-educated person if you had beautiful handwriting. Children copied wise sayings and Bible verses.

Choose a Bible verse below. In your best printing, copy the verse on the "slate." Remember: There were no lines to print on back then, so try to keep your writing straight and neat.

If God be for us, who can be against us? ~ Romans 8:31

Christ died for our sins. ~ 1 Corinthians 15:3

Learning to Read in 1874

Andi learns to read using McGuffey's readers. She will use McGuffey's readers until she finishes the eighth grade. There are six readers in all.

Make your own McGuffey's reader

Cut out the sample book pages on these three pages. Staple the pages together to make a book. Now you have an example of the kind of reader Andi and Cory used in 1874.

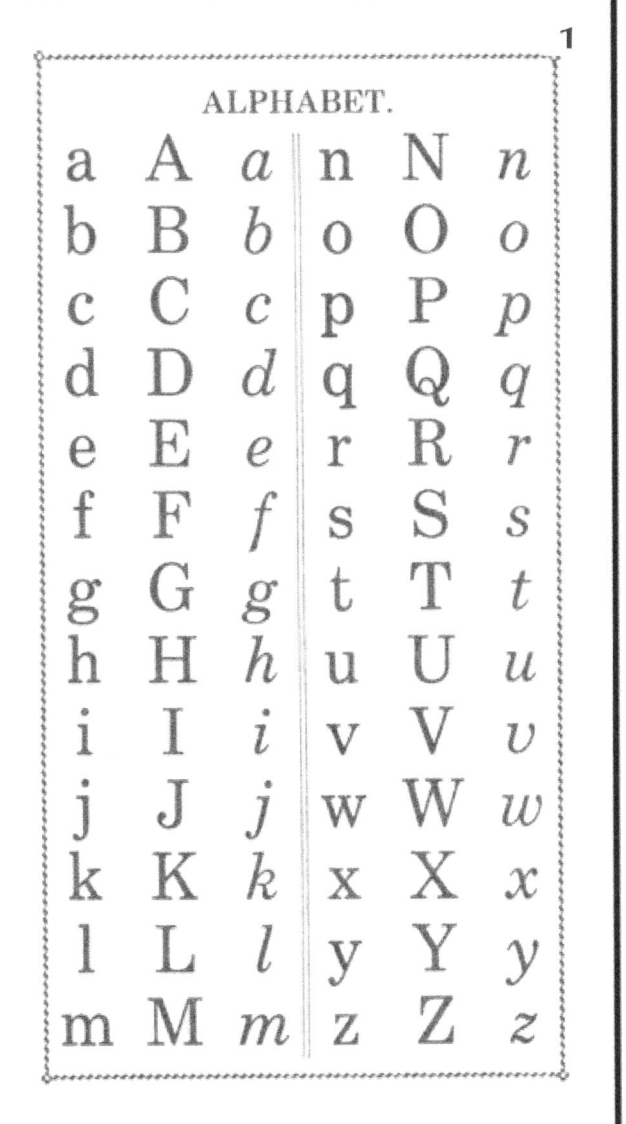

LESSON I.

Spelling.

is it an ox
it is an ox
it is my ox

Reading.

Is it an ox?
It is an ox.
It is my ox.

Spelling.

do we go
do we go up
we do go up

Reading. Do we go?
Do we go up?
We do go up.

Spelling.

am I in
am I in it
I am in it
so is he in it

Reading. Am I in?
Am I in it?
I am in it.
So is he in it.

LESSON II.*

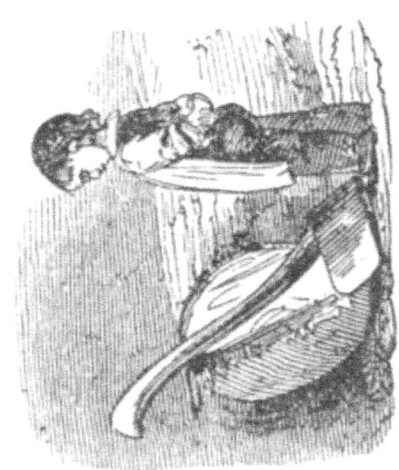

Is it an ax?
It is an ax.
It is my ax.
It is by me.
So it is!
I go to it.

* Let the child spell each word in the line; then read, as in Lesson 1.

LESSON I.

The New Book.

Here is John.

There are Ann and Jane.

Ann has a new book.

It is the first book.

Ann must keep it nice and clean.

LESSON II.

This boy has a bird.

This bird is on his hand.

Some birds can talk.

The dog barks.

Do you hear the dog bark?

Boys play with dogs.

The boys run fast.

They run as fast as they can.

One of the boys has no hat.

Here is a small dog.

He has the boy's hat.

The boys can not get it.

Andi's Scary School Days Chapters 7-9

Read the chapters and answer the questions.

Chapter 7- Runaway Lizard

1. The boys look for Pickles. Circle where the little lizard hides.

    behind the wood stove • in the corner • under Andi's desk

2. Who finds Pickles? _____

3. Why does Cory break the rule about brining pets to school?

    A. He does not know the rule.
    B. He knows Andi is lonely.
    C. He wants to show Pickles to his friends.

4. YES or NO (circle one)? Miss Hall lets Cory keep Pickles in the classroom.

Chapter 8- Runaway Pupil

5. Andi's big brother Justin works in a (circle one) . . .

    bank • newspaper office • law office • general store

6. What does Andi do keep Pickles from running away?

    _____

7. What happens after Andi runs away from school?

    A. She finds Justin.   B. She goes back to the ranch.   C. She gets lost.

Chapter 9- Horse Thief

8. YES or NO? The man in the barn thinks Andi wants to steal his horses.

9. The owner of the livery stable is Mr. Blake, _____ father.

10. After her big scare in the horse barn, what helps Andi feel better?

    A. cookies and milk   B. a hug from Justin   C. not returning to school

11. Who finds Andi at Cory's house? Melinda • Justin • Miss Hall

Fun with Words Chapters 7-9

The words in each of these sentences are mixed up. Can you unscramble them? Hint: Look on the page numbers to find the sentences in the book.

Hint: The first word of each sentence starts with a capital letter.

Example: hair yanked her Andi out ribbon. Andi yanked her hair ribbon out.

1. desk zipped the lizard teacher's under The. (page 49)

The _____

2. fence as post Andi still as sat a. (page 50)

Andi _____

3. busy looked Andi down and the up street. (page 56)

Andi _____

4. at horse up The backed touch her. (page 60)

The _____

5. above large her A stood man right. (page 62)

A _____

Your Turn!

Find a short sentence from chapters 7-9. Mix up the words. Write them here. Ask a parent, brother, or sister to unscramble the sentence. Could they do it? Write your mixed-up sentence here.

_____

Ask someone to write the unscrambled sentence here.

_____

Schoolhouse Maze

It's recess, and Andi can't find her way out of the schoolhouse. Can you help her? Follow the maze from Andi to the tree she climbs in the schoolyard. Do not cross any black lines.

Scary School Days Chapter 10 and A Peek into the Past

Read the chapters and answer the questions.

Chapter 10-Back to School

1. Andi tells three people she is sorry for running away. Who are they?

   _____   _____   _____

2. YES or NO (circle one)? Justin goes with Andi when she tells Miss Hall she is sorry for running away from the classroom.

3. What does Miss Hall let Andi do at the very end? _____

A Peek into the Past

4. Circle two ways teachers started school each morning in 1874.

   read the Bible • said the Pledge of Allegiance • sang a song

5. How old were the oldest pupils? _____

6. How old were the youngest pupils? _____

7. Write the number of swats for breaking these school rules in 1874.

   fighting: _____ • telling lies: _____ • calling others bad names: _____

Let's Write!

Circle your favorite animal character from *Andi's Scary School Days*.

   Taffy • the dead fly • Pickles the lizard • Thunder the horse

Write one sentence telling why this is your favorite animal. Draw your animal character in the box.

_____

_____

School Rules

Most schoolteachers were strict in the 1800s. There was often just one teacher for a lot of children of all ages. He or she had to keep the class in order. Parents felt the teacher was doing a good job if the class was quiet and well-behaved. That was more important in 1874 than if the children were learning. Parents liked a strict teacher.

- No talking
- Stay seated
- No turning around
- Raise your hand
- Sit up straight

Teachers had rules to obey too. They obeyed the rules the schoolboard set for them. They made pen tips for their pupils. They filled kerosene lamps. They brought in coal for the stove. Teachers spent their free time reading the Bible or other good books. Women teachers were not allowed to get married.

Would you like these rules if you went to school in 1874? Put an X in the "yes" or "no" boxes.

	YES	NO
1. Come to school with clean hands and face	☐	☐
2. Do not climb trees	☐	☐
3. Boys must not tease the girls	☐	☐
4. Boys and girls must play in different play areas	☐	☐
5. Keep your fingernails short	☐	☐
6. Do not leave your seat without permission	☐	☐
7. Do not turn around	☐	☐
8. Never be late for class	☐	☐
9. Do not throw anything in class	☐	☐
10. Do not splash in the water during playtime	☐	☐
11. Do not fight, lie, or cheat	☐	☐

Horse Colors

When Andi walked into the livery stable, she saw horses of many different colors. Horses come in all colors, and each color has a name.

Here are some names of horse colors and what they look like.

Color the horses below. Use these clues to choose what color each horse should be:

1. **Palomino** (pal-uh-mee-no): a gold-colored horse with a white mane and tail
2. **Bay**: a reddish-brown horse with a black mane and tail. It also has black lower legs
3. **Buckskin**: a light yellow horse with a black mane and tail. It has black lower legs. Sometimes a black stripe runs down its back
4. **Pinto**: a white horse with large black and brown spots on it
5. **Sorrel (Chestnut)**: a reddish-brown horse, with a reddish-brown mane and tail
6. **Black**: an all-black horse, with black mane and tail; it may have a white mark on its forehead

Palomino   Bay   Buckskin
Pinto   Sorrel   Black

Character Trait – Peaceful

Staying calm and reasonable even when things go wrong.

Psalm 46:10 says, **"Be still."** It means "stop fussing," or "stop being worried." There are many things to worry about, but we don't need to. Jesus wants his children to rest in Him and find peace.

Who Am I?

Look up the verses to learn who Jesus was telling to be at peace in these riddles.

1. (Mark 4:39) I gave Jesus's disciples a lot of fear and worry. I blew hard. I splashed big waves over the boat. I made things very scary. Jesus told me to stop, and I obeyed. Who am I? _____

2. (John 14:27) We followed Jesus everywhere for three years and were His close friends. When He told us He would soon leave us, we were scared. Who are we? _____

3. (Matthew 11:28-29) We listened to Jesus and liked what we heard. We were restless and worried, but Jesus spoke peace to us. Who are we? _____

Schedule for Book 5: Andi's Lonely Little Foal

*indicates an optional activity found in the *Andi's Lonely Little Foal* lapbook.
(Lapbook activities **can be skipped** or purchased at AndiandTaffy.com)

Lonely Little Foal	Day 1	Day 2	Day 3	Day 4
Book	"New Words" & Chapter 1	Chapter 2	———	Chapter 3
Activities	Page 85 #1-4	Page 85 #5-8	*Lapbook activity Chapters 1-2 & Lapbook cover*	Page 85 #9-13
Lonely Little Foal	**Day 5**	**Day 6**	**Day 7**	**Day 8**
Book	———	———	Chapter 4	———
Activities	Pages 86-87	Pages 88-89	Page 90 #1-4	*Lapbook activity Chapters 3-4 (#1)*
Lonely Little Foal	**Day 9**	**Day 10**	**Day 11**	**Day 12**
Book	———	Chapter 5	Chapter 6	———
Activities	*Lapbook activity Chapters 3-4 (#2)*	Page 90 #5-8	Page 90 #9-11	*Lapbook activity Chapters 5-6 (#1)*
Lonely Little Foal	**Day 13**	**Day 14**	**Day 15**	**Day 16**
Book	———	———	———	Chapter 7
Activities	*Lapbook activity Chapters 5-6 (#2)*	Pages 91-92	Pages 93-97	Page 99 #1-4
Lonely Little Foal	**Day 17**	**Day 18**	**Day 19**	**Day 20**
Book	Chapter 8	———	Chapter 9	———
Activities	Page 99 #5-8	*Lapbook activity Chapters 7-8*	Page 99 #9-12	Pages 100-101
Lonely Little Foal	**Day 21**	**Day 22**	**Day 23**	**Day 24**
Book	Chapter 10	———	A Peek into the Past	———
Activities	Page 102 #1-4	*Lapbook activity Chapters 9-10*	Page 102 #5 and Let's Write!	Page 103

Andi's Lonely Little Foal Chapters 1-3

Read the chapters and answer the questions.

Chapter 1- The Not-So-Good Idea

1. What does Andi like to daydream about?

    A. going to school   B. riding Taffy   C. playing with Riley

2. What do YOU like to daydream about? _____
_____

3. What mean boy is filling Andi's thoughts? _____

4. YES or NO (circle one)? Andi is big enough to make decisions about Taffy.

Chapter 2- Taffy

5. YES or NO (circle one)? Andi is excited about helping Chad with Taffy.

6. Who will collect the eggs for Andi today? _____

7. How old is Andi's friend Riley? _____ How old is Andi? _____

8. Andi makes the right words come out to say to Chad. What does she say?

   A. "I'm sorry I got mad."   B. "You are not the boss!"   C. "I want to help."

Chapter 3- Lasso Fun

9. YES or NO (circle one)? Andi's chore for the day is playing with Taffy.

10. Which horse must Andi keep Taffy from going near?

    A. Coco   B. Midnight   C. Snowflake

11. What are the names of the 3 ranch dogs?

_____ _____ _____

12. Why does Riley call the ranch dogs?

A. He wants to play. B. He wants to lasso them. C. He wants to feed them.

13. Circle the dog Riley lassos with his rope.   Prince • King • Duke

New Words Chapters 1-3

Look at the New Words list on page 7 to find the word that fits.

1. Taffy gave a happy _____ when she saw Andi.

    (a friendly horse greeting)

2. Taffy _____ Andi's shoulder. She nibbled Andi's hair.

    (when a horse rubs or pushes gently with its nose)

More Fun with New Words

Circle the meaning of each underlined word in these sentences.

3. Andi <u>perked up</u>. A penny could buy lemon drops. Or taffy candy.

    Perked up means . . .   A. became cheerful   B. cried   C. laughed

4. "Johnny is a <u>bully</u>," Melinda said.

    A bully is . . .   A. a big boy   B. a mean, bossy person   C. a grown-up

5. Duke <u>nipped</u> Coco's legs and barked.

    Nipped means . . .   A. took a small bite   B. pinched   C. grabbed

6. "Chad will <u>skin you alive</u> if you try to rope a calf," Andi said.

    Skin you alive means . . .   A. spank you   B. laugh at you   C. yell at you

Andi has her lasso and she's ready to rope an animal. She even has Pickles in her pocket to help her lasso. Draw the animal you think might be a good one for Andi to lasso!

Where Do You Live?

Write the name of the state where you live. _____

On the map below, color your state red.

Name two states that border (touch) your state. Color these states blue. Write their names: _____ _____

If your state does *not* border two other states, write what *does* touch your state (Atlantic Ocean, Pacific Ocean, Canada, or Mexico).

Andi lives in California. Name two states that border (touch) California.

_____ _____

A Penny for Your Thoughts

In Chapter 1, Andi did not know what Justin meant when he said, "A penny for your thoughts." People talked a little differently in the 1800s and out West. It sounds funny to hear these idioms (id-ee-ums) today. Can you figure out what these 1800s cowboys and cowgirls are saying?

Find the letter at the bottom of the page that matches each idiom. Write the letter next to the idiom. The first one has been done for you.

Indian head penny

__D__ 1. The sheriff had never seen so many **shooting irons** at one time.

_____ 2. Riley was all **tuckered out** after doing his chores.

_____ 3. Johnny thinks he is the **biggest frog in the puddle.**

_____ 4. Mitch did a **bang-up** job fixing the fence.

_____ 5. Riley got into **a heap of trouble** for roping the calf.

_____ 6. Johnny was **shooting off his mouth**, so Andi pulled his hair.

_____ 7. Mother **had a conniption fit** when she saw how dirty Andi was.

_____ 8. Andi got **slicked up** for the first day of school.

* * * *

A. most important person of all

B. was very upset

C. great; excellent

D. ~~guns and rifles~~

E. worn out; tired

F. big trouble

G. dressed up nice

H. being sassy; talking without thinking

A Lonely Foal

Foals do not like to be taken away from their mothers. Andi's foal did not like to be taken away either. Can you help Taffy find her way back to Snowflake? Do not cross any black lines.

89

Andi's Lonely Little Foal Chapters 4-6

Read the chapters and answer the questions.

Chapter 4- Lasso Trouble

1. What is Riley's cowboy yell? _____

2. Which part of the calf does Riley lasso? _____

3. What does Riley lose?   A. his rope   B. his britches   C. his boots

4. Who gets mad at Riley for lassoing the calf?   Chad • Uncle Sid • Cook

Chapter 5- Up, Up, and Over!

5. YES or NO (circle one)? Taffy jumps over the fence to be with Snowflake.

6. What does Riley say Andi should do?   A. tell Chad what happened

   B. take Taffy back to her stall   C. put Snowflake back in her pasture

7. What does Taffy do every time Andi leaves? _____

8. Circle the treats Andi brings Taffy to help her feel better.

   apples   •   grass   •   sugar   •   carrots   •   grain

Chapter 6- Night Noises

9. Andi has to trust _____ that he is doing the best thing for Taffy.

10. What makes the *scratch, scratch, scratch* noise in the barn? _____

11. The grandfather clock bongs _____ times. What time is it?

   Write the digital time. Draw the hands on the clock.

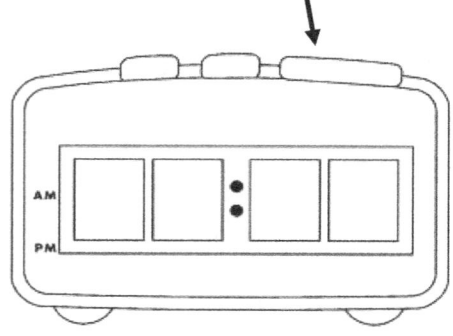 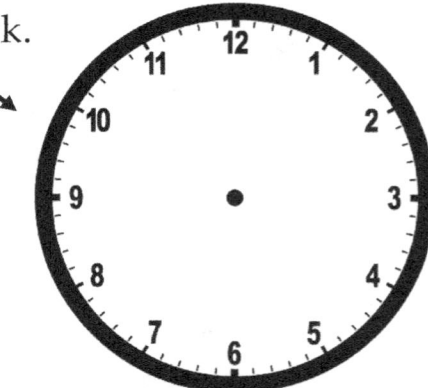

90

New Words for Chapters 4-6

Word Match- Draw a line between the words and what they mean. If you need help, look at the New Words list on page 7 in *Lonely Little Foal*.

bellow • seeds like corn and oats; food for cows and horses

grain • a horse's or cow's feet

grandfather clock • to make a loud, deep noise

hooves • a tall clock that stands on the floor

señorita • what the cowboys yell to round up the cattle

yippee-ki-yay! • the Spanish word for "miss"

More Fun with New Words

Use the words from the word box and the clues to fill in the missing words in these sentences from chapters 4-6.

1. Andi _____. "Are you sure you can rope that calf?" (swallowed hard)

2. Andi _____ up on Coco and kicked him. (climbed fast)

3. Cook was finding _____ of chores for Riley. (lots and lots)

4. Andi closed her eyes. The straw _____ under her. (swished)

5. Everything felt warm and _____ now. (snug; peaceful)

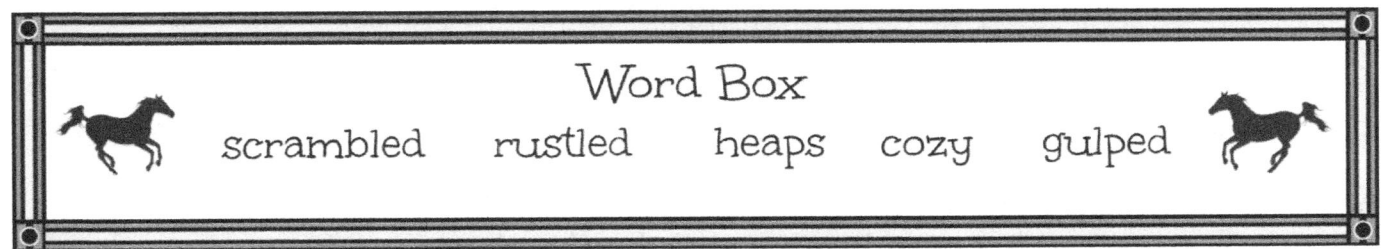

Word Box

scrambled   rustled   heaps   cozy   gulped

What Does a Cowboy Wear?

Riley lassos a calf. He is a cowboy.

The cowboy on the left is dressed for work. Each piece of clothing has a purpose. Read about the different pieces of clothing a cowboy needs and then color each piece. (You need colored pencils for this activity.)

A cowboy needs a . . .

Hat–A cowboy's hat shades him from the sun. It is an umbrella in the rain. He also uses his hat as a bucket to scoop up water for himself or his horse. **Color the hat brown.**

Boots–Boots keep the cowboy's feet safe from stickers, brush, and even snakes. They are narrow and have a high heel, to keep the boot in the stirrup. **Color the boots black.**

Shirt–The cowboy's shirt is always long-sleeved to protect his arms. He wears cotton shirts in the summer and wool shirts in the winter. **Color the shirt red.**

Bandana–This is a square piece of cloth, folded in half like a triangle. The cowboy keeps it around his neck. He uses it to keep the dust out of his mouth and nose. He can wet it to keep cool or use it as a bandage if he starts to bleed. **Color the bandana orange.**

Vest–A cowboy's shirt and pants often do not have pockets. A vest has a lot of pockets to keep money, a knife, and other valuables. **Color the vest blue.**

Pants–These are made of heavy denim or wool. There is one small pocket at the waist or none at all. It's hard to reach into a pants pocket while riding a horse. You don't need to color the pants because they are under the . . .

Chaps–Leather leggings fit over the pants to protect the cowboy from rocks, brush, and cows' horns. They help keep him warm too. **Color the chaps brown.**

Gloves– Made of leather, gloves protect the cowboy's hands from rope burns, blisters, hooves, and hot branding irons. **Color the gloves green.**

Saddle Your Horse

Andi and Riley ride their horses bareback. This means they ride without saddles. But a cowboy usually puts a saddle on his horse, along with reins and a bridle. A cowboy also makes sure he has his lasso on his saddle. He hangs his canteen around his saddle horn. Sometimes he carries saddlebags and a bedroll.

➢ Color the horse your favorite horse colors. Color the background too.
➢ Cut out the horse "tack" on pages 95-97 and paste them on the horse.
➢ Cut around the picture on the dotted line.

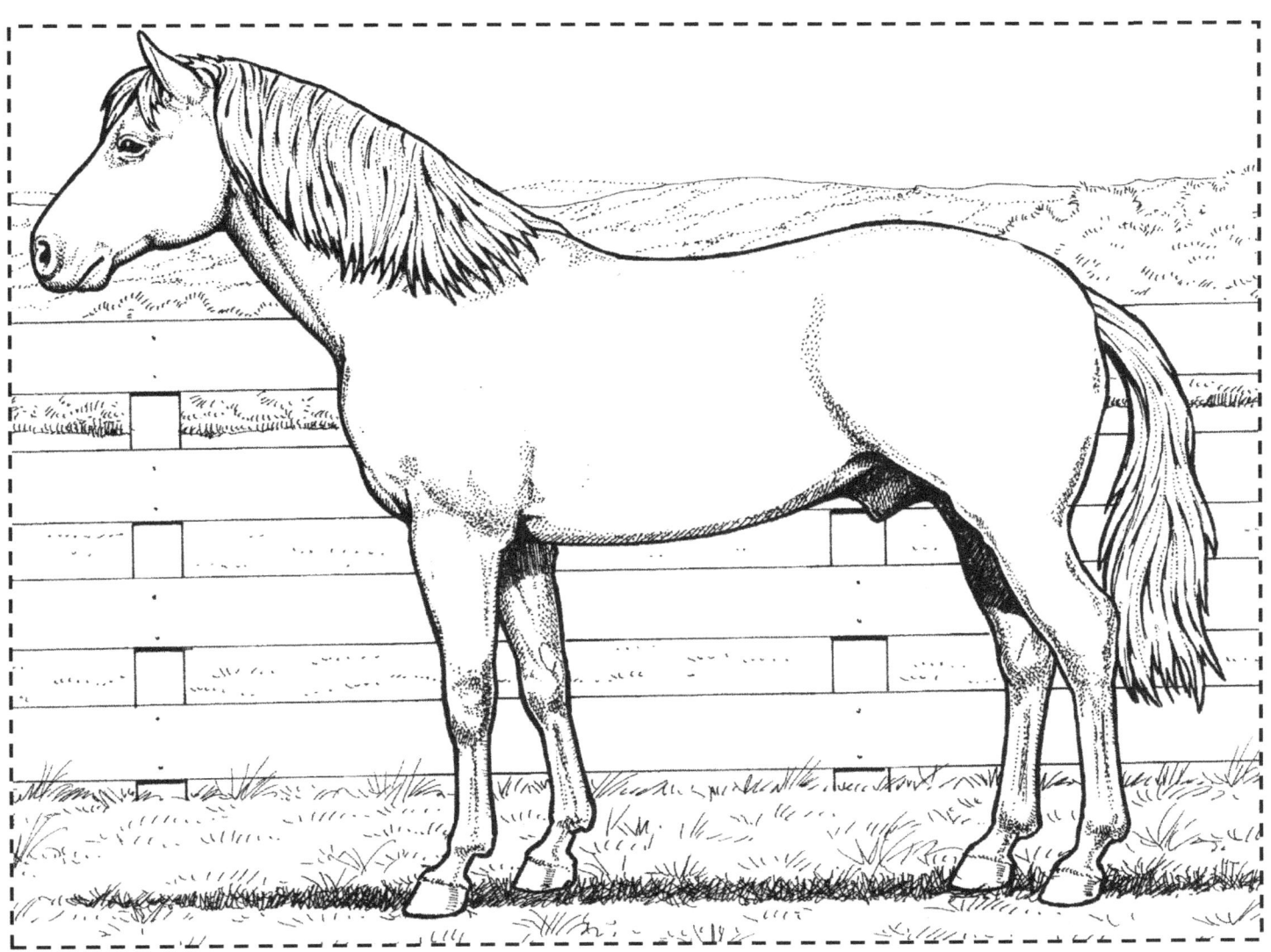

Horse Tack

"Tack" is the word for the gear that goes on a horse. It is very important to tack up a horse correctly. Each piece has a special job. On this page and the next are pieces of tack that go on a horse to get him ready to ride. **Read what each piece of tack is for. Then color them, cut them out, and paste them on your horse.**

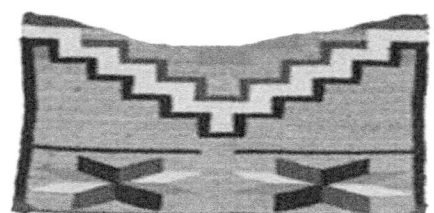

The **SADDLE BLANKET** goes on first. It is soft. It keeps the saddle from rubbing against the horse and making him sore. Always make sure the blanket is smooth, with no wrinkles, before putting the saddle on top of it.

Note: When you paste the saddle on, leave the saddle horn free so you can slip the lasso around it later.

The **SADDLE** is the seat for the cowboy. Some days, a cowboy sits in his saddle all day. It must be comfortable. A saddle is made from leather. It has a "horn" that sticks up at the front. The horn can hold the cowboy's lasso or canteen. "Stirrups" hang down. That's where the cowboy puts his feet. "Saddle strings" are thin, leather strings that hang down from the saddle. The cowboy can tie things up with them, like a bedroll (sleeping bag). The "cinch" is a belt that goes around and under the horse's belly. The cinch keeps the saddle on the horse. It must be pulled tight or the saddle may slip off. A horse does not like having that cinch on. Sometimes he sucks in air and pushes his stomach out so the cinch cannot get tight. Later, when the horse lets his breath out, the saddle will become too loose. Always make sure your saddle is cinched up tight!

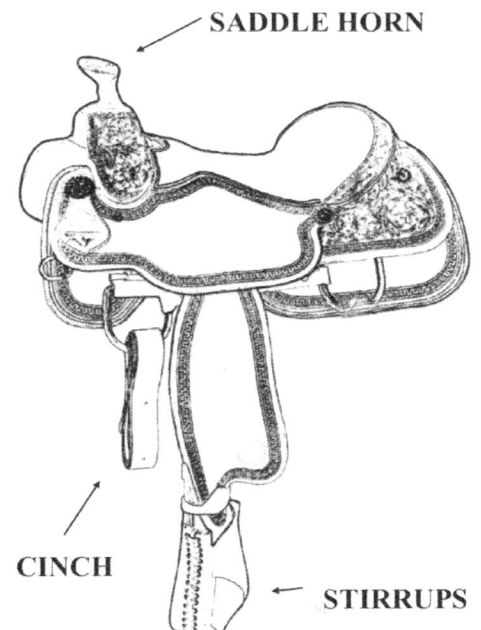

Horse Tack

LASSO (rope) is one of the cowboy's most important tools. It hangs down from his saddle, right by the saddle horn. He uses it to catch horses, cows, and calves. A cowboy can be galloping on his horse and throw his lasso perfectly! The lasso can also hang around the saddle horn. Cut out the lasso (and the inside also). Now, try to slip this lasso around the saddle horn on your picture. Be careful! Don't rip the saddle horn off!

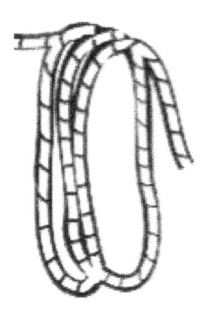

The headgear controls the horse. The **BRIDLE** goes around the horse's head. It holds the **BIT** and the **REINS**. The bit is a metal bar the horse holds in his mouth. The cowboy uses the two long reins—which are connected to the bit—to tell the horse where to go. The bit is tiny, but it makes the horse obey. If the cowboy wants to go left, he pulls left on the reins. If he wants the horse to stop, he pulls back on the reins.

Use this picture of a horse's head to figure out where the bridle and reins go.
Now, draw a bridle and reins on your horse.

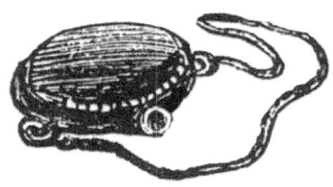

A **CANTEEN** holds water. The cowboy hangs it from his saddle or around the saddle horn.

SADDLE BAGS carry extra supplies, like the cowboy's lunch. Saddle bags hang over the sides of the horse, just behind the saddle.

A **BEDROLL** is the cowboy's blanket. If the cowboy sleeps outside on the ground, he needs his bedroll. He rolls it up and carries it with the saddlebags, just behind the saddle.

Andi's Lonely Little Foal Chapters 7-9

Read the chapters and answer the questions.

Chapter 7- Sunday Is Not a School Day

1. Who wakes Andi up Sunday morning? _____

2. Circle the things Andi likes about Sunday school. Cross out what she
   does not like: Johnny • the Bible story • leaving Taffy • the songs
   • her Sunday school teacher • going to "school" on Sunday

3. What new song does Andi learn? _____

4. YES or NO? God cares about little prayer requests as much as big ones.

Chapter 8- That Mean Johnny

5. What does Johnny shoot from his slingshot? _____

6. What does Andi want to do to mean Johnny?

   A. pull his hair   B. spit on him   C. punch him

7. When you take a baby horse from its mother, it is called _____.

8. YES or NO (circle one)? Johnny tells Andi that baby Taffy might die.

Chapter 9- Taffy Trouble

9. Why doesn't Andi want to drive the buggy home?

   A. her hands hurt   B. her hands are too shaky   C. she's afraid to drive

10. How do you think Taffy got hurt?

    A. Johnny cut her.   B. Taffy bumped into her stall wall.   C. Taffy fell down.

11. Circle the things that keep Andi awake when she is in the barn.

    it's cold • an owl hoots • it rains • the cats hiss • a coyote howls

12. Who wakes Andi up on this school morning? _____

New Words Chapters 7-9

Circle the meaning of each underlined word in the sentences.

1. *Whiz!* An <u>acorn</u> flew from Johnny's slingshot.

    An acorn is . . .   A. a kind of nut   B. a pebble   C. a hard vegetable seed

2. Andi <u>squinted</u> at that mean boy.

    Squinted means . . .   A. laughed   B. narrowed her eyes   C. ignored

3. Andi <u>slumped</u> against Taffy.

    Slumped means . . .   A. brushed   B. walked   C. fell

4. *Whack!* She <u>slammed</u> into Riley.

    Slammed means . . .   A. crashed   B. tripped   C. ran around

5. Taffy <u>nuzzled</u> Andi's neck and nibbled her hair.

    Nuzzled means . . .   A. nipped   B. snuggled   C. breathed on

What Am I?

Read the riddles and draw pictures for your answers. Use the word box.

6. That mean Johnny uses me to shoot acorns.

7. I am something to sit on. I do not have a back.

8. I am what a rancher burns into his calves.

Word Box

brandmark   bench   slingshot

100

The Song "Jesus Loves Me"

Andi learned a new song in Sunday school called "Jesus Loves Me." Even though the song was new to Andi, it had already been around for 12 years. A woman named Anna B. Warner wrote "Jesus Loves Me" as a poem in 1860. Two years later, in 1862, a man named William Bradbury found the poem in a book and created a tune to go along with the words. "Jesus Loves Me" is the most-loved and best-known hymn in the world. Listen to "Jesus Loves Me" at this link: **CircleCBooks.com/beginnings/**

Jesus loves me this I know.
For the Bible tells me so.
Little ones to Him belong.
They are weak but He is strong.

Chorus:
Yes, Jesus loves me.
Yes, Jesus loves me.
Yes, Jesus loves me.
The Bible tells me so.

Trace over the first word of each line. Then copy the rest of the first verse.

Jesus _____

For _____

Little _____

They _____

Lonely Little Foal Chapter 10 and A Peek into the Past

Read the chapters and answer the questions.

Chapter 10- Trust Me!

1. Why does Andi feel terrible on the ride home from school?

    A. Johnny hurt her on the playground.

    B. Melinda is teasing her.

    C. Andi has disobeyed Chad.

2. Who tells Andi that Chad has taken Taffy away? _____

3. YES or NO (circle one)? When Andi tells Chad she is sorry for not trusting him, Chad brings Taffy home right away.

4. What is the name of Chad's horse? _____

A Peek into the Past

5. Circle three things you learned about cowboys in 1874.

   They made lots of money. • They slept in the bunkhouse. • They worked hard.
   All cowboys had guns. • They fixed fences. • They worked a few hours a day.

Let's Write!

Pretend you are a cowboy or cowgirl. What would be your favorite job on a ranch? Write two sentences. The first sentence tells your favorite job. The next sentence tells why it is your favorite job. Use capital letters and periods.

My favorite job would be _____

_____

_____

_____

Character Trait – Boldness

Believing that what I say or do is right in God's eyes, no matter what others think.

Boldness

Memorizing God's Word can help you become bold for Jesus.

I can do all things through Him [Christ] who strengthens me. Philippians 4:13

It can be scary to speak up for Jesus, especially when you are the only one doing it. But if you ask Him, God will give you the confidence to speak boldly!

Unscramble the mixed-up letters in the words below to learn when and where you should be bold to say or do what is right and true in God's sight.

Word Box
faith   school   lie   playground   pray   home   friends   steal

1. When somebody tells me I cannot **rapy.** _____

2. When I am on the **drounpgyal.** _____

3. When I am with my **driensf.** _____

4. When somebody makes fun of my **taihf.** _____

5. When I am at **mhoe.** _____

6. When I am at **looshc.** _____

7. When somebody asks me to **eil** for them. _____

8. When someone wants me to **tlsea.** _____

Schedule for Book 6: **Andi's Circle C Christmas**

*indicates an optional activity found in the *Andi's Circle C Christmas* lapbook.
(Lapbook activities **can be skipped** or purchased at AndiandTaffy.com)

Circle C Christmas	Day 1	Day 2	Day 3	Day 4
Book	"New Words" & Chapter 1	Chapter 2	———	———
Activities	Page 105 #1-3	Page 105 #4-6	*Lapbook activity Chapters 1-2 (#1) & Lapbook cover	*Lapbook activity Chapters 1-2 (#2)
Circle C Christmas	**Day 5**	**Day 6**	**Day 7**	**Day 8**
Book	Chapter 3	———	———	Chapter 4
Activities	Page 105 #7-11	Pages 106-107	Pages 108-109	Page 110 #1-3
Circle C Christmas	**Day 9**	**Day 10**	**Day 11**	**Day 12**
Book	———	Chapter 5	Chapter 6	———
Activities	*Lapbook activity Chapters 3-4	Page 110 #4-7	Page 110 #8-10	*Lapbook activity Chapters 5-6
Circle C Christmas	**Day 13**	**Day 14**	**Day 15**	**Day 16**
Book	———	Chapter 7	Chapter 8	———
Activities	Pages 111-112	Page 113 #1-3	Page 113 #4-7	*Lapbook activity Chapters 7-8
Circle C Christmas	**Day 17**	**Day 18**	**Day 19**	**Day 20**
Book	Chapter 9	———	Chapter 10	———
Activities	Page 113 #8-10	Pages 114-115	Page 116 #1-3	*Lapbook activity Chapters 9-10
Circle C Christmas	**Day 21**	**Day 22**	**Day 23**	**Day 24**
Book	A Peek into the Past	———	———	———
Activities	Page 116 #4-6 and Let's Write!	Pages 117-118	*Lapbook activity 5 story elements	Pages 119-121

Andi's Circle C Christmas Chapters 1-3

Read the chapters and answer the questions.

Chapter 1- A Fly on a Leash

1. The setting is where the story takes place. Where are Andi and Riley playing when this story begins? _____

2. Riley catches a _____ for Pickles the lizard.

3. YES or NO (circle one)? Riley lives on the ranch with his Uncle Sid because his mother is sick.

Chapter 2- Christmas Lists

4. Andi's list is not correct. Cross out the words that do not belong.

5. YES or NO (circle one)? Pickles eats the fly Andi brings into the house.

6. Who knocks on the front door?

_____

sling shot   doll
harmonica
knife   lasso
brush for Taffy
hair ribbon
new dress

Chapter 3- Surprise!

7. YES or NO (circle one)? Mother knows Aunt Rebecca was coming to help.

8. What is Mother's first name? _____

9. How did Aunt Rebecca get out to the ranch?

   A. She took the train.   B. She drove a buggy.   C. She walked.

10. Aunt Rebecca scolds Mother for letting Andi . . . (circle three)

    talk back • play with a boy • shout • wear overalls • keep a lizard

11. Which word describes Aunt Rebecca?   A. quiet   B. nervous   C. bossy

New Words Chapters 1-3

Word Match- Draw a line between the words and what they mean. If you need help, look at the New Words list on page 7 in *Circle C Christmas*.

carpetbag • to use yarn to make things like a sweater or a scarf

fort • perfume that smells like roses

hankie • an old-fashioned suitcase; a travel bag made out of carpet

knit • an army base where soldiers live and work

rose water • a big city in California near the Pacific Ocean

San Francisco • a square piece of cloth used for wiping the eyes or nose; a handkerchief

More Fun with New Words

Use the words from the word box and the clues to fill in the missing words in these sentences from chapters 1-3.

1. That gold piece was a _____ treasure. (one-of-a-kind)

2. Andi _____ her list in her pocket. (shoved)

3. Aunt Rebecca didn't wait for Andi to _____ her in. (ask)

4. "Get rid of that animal this very _____!" (second)

5. Andi's heart was _____ fast. (beating)

Word Box
special   invite   thumping   stuffed   instant

Blue Belly Lizards

Andi's lizard, Pickles, is a blue belly lizard. It is also called a western fence lizard. Blue belly lizards are easy to find in California. They grow to a nice "pet" size, up to 6 or 7 inches long (from nose to tail).

Blue belly lizards are brown or black in color, with tan or green-blue markings. But the prettiest color on the male (boy) lizard is its bright-blue belly.

Blue belly lizards like to sun themselves on rocks and high places, like fence posts. This makes them an easy meal for snakes and birds. The lizards are fast, however, and can change color to fool the birds.

A blue belly lizard makes a good pet. All you need is a big box with dirt and climbing sticks, a heat source, water, and insects. The lizard eats crickets, ants, spiders, and other small bugs. A blue belly lizard can be trained to lie quietly in your hands. It likes the warmth of your body and will fall asleep.

Color Pickles. Color Pickles in his box. He is a male lizard, so his belly should be blue. Draw some bugs and a dish of water. Add sticks and dirt.
See a real blue belly lizard being tamed in this 1 ½ minute video at this link:

CircleCBooks.com/beginnings/

Where Is San Francisco?

Aunt Rebecca lives in a big house in the city of San Francisco, California. Riley's father is a soldier at the fort in San Francisco too. In 1874, San Francisco was the biggest city in the West. More than 150,000 (one hundred fifty thousand) people lived there.

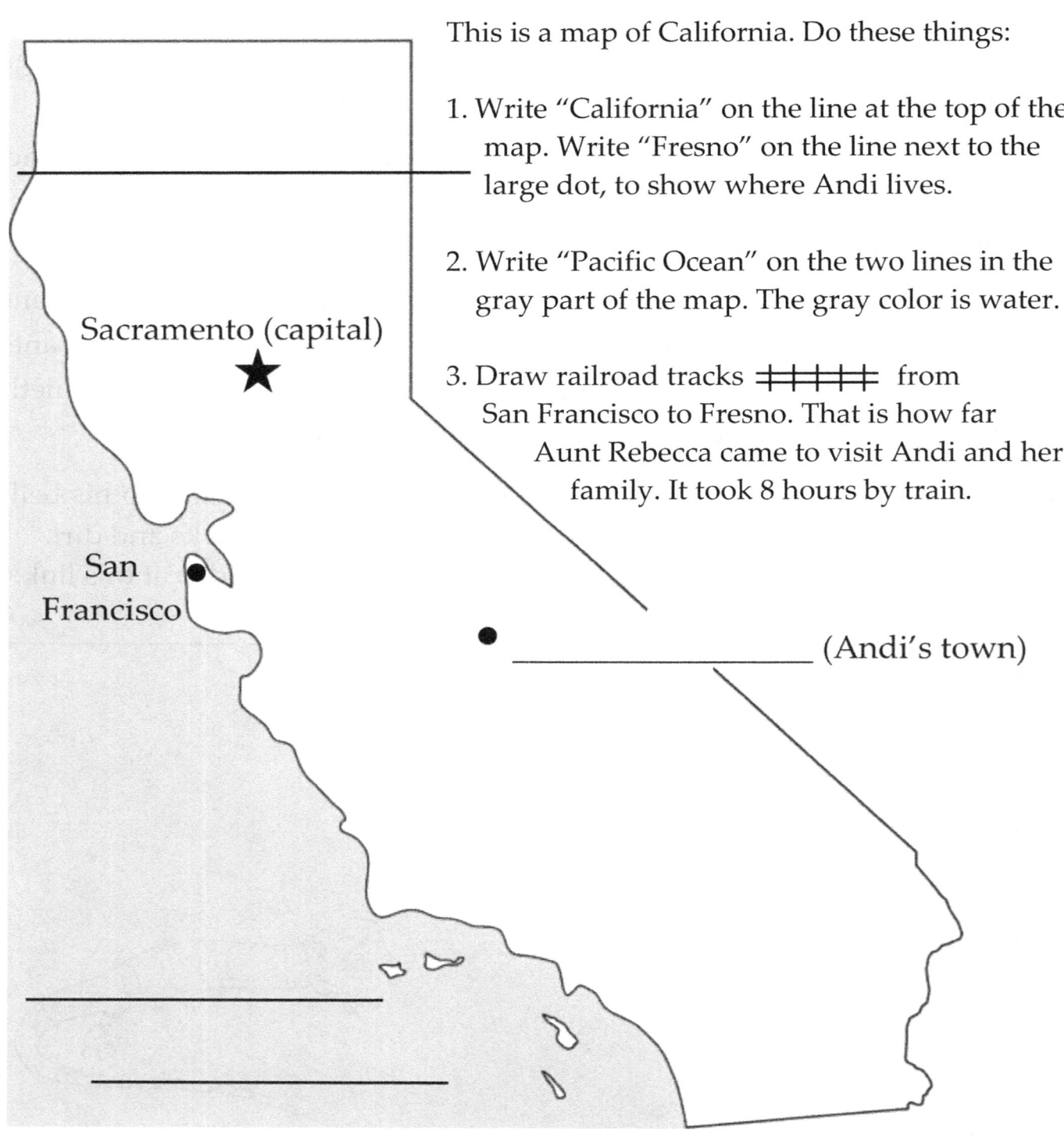

This is a map of California. Do these things:

1. Write "California" on the line at the top of the map. Write "Fresno" on the line next to the large dot, to show where Andi lives.

2. Write "Pacific Ocean" on the two lines in the gray part of the map. The gray color is water.

3. Draw railroad tracks ┼┼┼┼ from San Francisco to Fresno. That is how far Aunt Rebecca came to visit Andi and her family. It took 8 hours by train.

The Fort in San Francisco

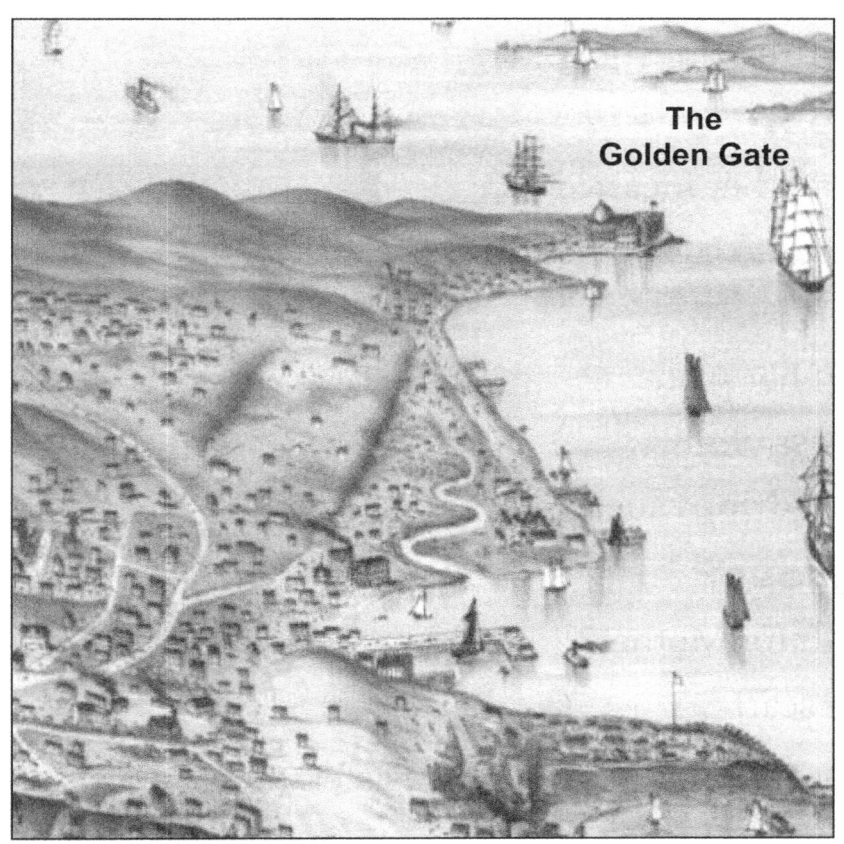

Riley wants to go home to San Francisco for Christmas. Home is the Presidio (pre-SEE-dee-o), an army fort in the city. Riley's father is a captain there. This map shows a small part of San Francisco in 1874. Look at all the ships in the bay! They are coming to the big city to buy and sell goods. The Presidio sits on land sticking out near the top of the map, right below the "Golden Gate."

<u>**Draw a circle around the Presidio**</u>.

The Spanish built the Presidio in 1776. The United States got the fort in 1847. Today, the Presidio is a big park near the **Golden Gate Bridge**. There was no bridge in 1874. The waterway was called "The Golden Gate." Much later, a bridge was built. It was named after the waterway—"Golden Gate Bridge."

On the map, <u>**draw a bridge**</u> over the water at the Golden Gate. Here is what the Golden Gate Bridge looks like today. The empty hills on the map are covered with buildings. What color is the bridge? Unscramble the letters. **DRE**

_____

109

Andi's Circle C Christmas Chapters 4-6

Read the chapters and answer the questions.

Chapter 4- Supper Guest

1. Who wants to help Andi cut up her meat? _____

2. What happens when Andi tries to cut up her meat?

    A. She cuts her finger.

    B. She knocks the meat off her plate.

    C. She knocks over her glass of milk.

3. Whose dinner plate ends up a drippy mess? _____

Chapter 5- Who's the Boss?

4. What is Andi knitting as a gift for Mother?

    A. a pot holder   B. a scarf   C. a hat

5. Aunt Rebecca is Father's   OLDER • YOUNGER   sister. (circle one)

6. What is Andi's full name?

_____ _____ _____
     FIRST NAME   MIDDLE NAME   LAST NAME

7. What is your full name?

_____ _____ _____
     FIRST NAME   MIDDLE NAME   LAST NAME

Chapter 6- Mud and Coco

8. What does Andi ask God to help her do when Aunt Rebecca bosses her?

    A. to not talk back to Aunt Rebecca   C. to make Aunt Rebecca happy

    B. to obey Aunt Rebecca   D. all of these things

9. What is hanging over the back of Andi's chair? a coat • a lasso • an apron

10. Aunt Rebecca says Taffy will be trained to do something when she grows up. What is it? _____

New Words Chapters 4-6

Turn back to page 7 in *Circle C Christmas* and find the words below. Write what each word means. Use your best printing.

1. **company** _____

2. **spoil** _____

_____

More Fun with New Words

Circle the meaning of each underlined word in these sentences.

3. "Don't <u>slouch</u>, Andrea," Aunt Rebecca said.

    Slouch means . . .   A. hunch over   B. fall down   C. talk back

4. Andi <u>jabbed</u> her knife into the big chunk and started sawing.

    Jabbed means . . .   A. nudged   B. sneaked   C. poked

5. "Mother would be so <u>ashamed</u>!"

    Ashamed means . . .   A. happy   B. embarrassed   C. angry

6. Andi prayed in a <u>rush</u>.

    Rush means . . .   A. in a hurry   B. in a bad mood   C. in tears

Draw a Picture

7. Some words draw pictures in your mind like "Her hands were as cold as ice." Draw a picture for this sentence:

Andi felt as stiff as a fence post.

Story Characters

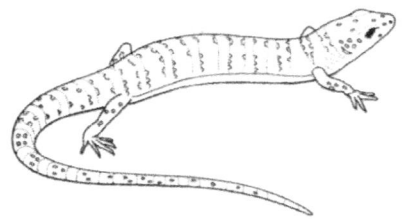

You have met a lot of characters in *Andi's Circle C Christmas*. Can you remember who they are? Draw a line from the characters to their descriptions.

Andi • Andi's oldest brother. He offers to cut up her meat.

Riley • The main character in *Circle C Christmas*.

Justin • Andi's friend, who lives on the ranch while his mother is sick.

Aunt Rebecca • Andi's grumpy aunt from San Francisco. She doesn't like spiders.

Chad • Andi's big sister. She helps Andi make a Christmas present for their mother.

Taffy • The pony Andi rides while wearing her new dress.

Coco • Andi's other big brother. She thinks he is bossy.

Melinda • Riley's uncle. He is the ranch foreman (boss).

Uncle Sid • Andi's lizard. He loves to eat spiders and flies.

Pickles • Andi's foal.

Andi's Circle C Christmas Chapters 7-9

Read the chapters and answer the questions.

Chapter 7- Riley

1. Who rescues Andi from Aunt Rebecca's scolding?

    A. Justin   B. Chad   C. Melinda

2. Riley finds a lot of _____ in the corner of the barn. Count them. How many are there? _____

3. What is Andi hiding behind her back? _____

Chapter 8-Buggy Ride

4. Four people see the broken jar of spiders. Circle the only person who was NOT shrieking.   Aunt Rebecca • Mother • Melinda • Andi

5. Circle the names of the people who went to town shopping. Put a box around those who stayed home and baked cookies. Cross out the others.

    Melinda • Mother • Mitch • Aunt Rebecca • Andi • Riley

6. YES or NO? Andi is very excited to go to a tea party with Aunt Rebecca.

7. What falls off the buggy? _____

Chapter 9- Andi's Best Idea

8. Why is Andi scared? Circle the four reasons. • Andi broke her arm • Aunt Rebecca bumped her head • it's raining • Andi is cold and wet a dog scares her • it will be dark soon • they have nothing to eat

9. What is Andi's best idea ever? _____

10. YES or NO (circle one)? Aunt Rebecca thinks it is a great idea too.

New Words Chapters 7-9

Match the words with the means. See page 7 in *Circle C Christmas*.

1. **harness** • to connect a horse to a buggy so the horse can pull it

2. **hitch** • the straps and other gear that hold a horse to the buggy

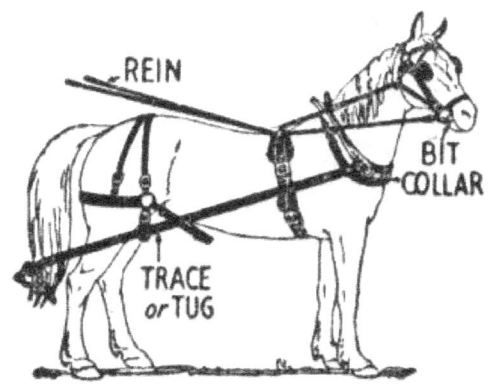

See an old-fashioned buggy at this link (25 seconds).
CircleCBooks.com/beginnings/

More Fun with New Words

Circle the meaning of each underlined word in these sentences.

3. "Good morning, Aunt Rebecca," Chad said in a <u>cheery</u> voice.

   Cheery means . . . A. happy B. tired C. sad

4. Andi <u>zipped</u> away from Aunt Rebecca as fast as a jackrabbit.

   Zipped means . . . A. jumped B. ran fast C. skipped

5. Aunt Rebecca's <u>screechy</u> voice stopped Andi in her tracks.

   Screechy means . . . A. high-pitched B. quiet C. angry

6. Aunt Rebecca is not used to such a <u>lively</u> little girl like Andi.

   Lively means . . . A. young B. quiet C. energetic

7. Suddenly, the buggy gave a great big <u>lurch</u>.

   Lurch means . . . A. a fall B. a jerk C. a noise

What's Different?

When Aunt Rebecca comes, Andi sometimes hides in the barn. Sometimes she goes to the pond to escape her aunt's bossing. Here are two pictures of Andi at the pond. Eight things are not the same in picture 2. Circle the things that are different. The first one has been done you.

Circle C Christmas Chapter 10 and A Peek into the Past

Read the chapters and answer the questions.

Chapter 10- Home for Christmas

1. Circle the things Aunt Rebecca does when she rides Pal.

    • she screams • she tells Andi to stop • she loses her hat • she gets wet

2. Where do Andi and Aunt Rebecca land when Pal stops too fast?

   _____

3. What is the special Christmas present Uncle Sid brings Riley?

   _____

A Peek into the Past

4. Christmas trees in 1874 did not have any electric lights because they were

    A. too expensive   B. too dangerous   C. not invented yet

5. What did people use instead of electric lights? _____

6. List four things children used to decorate the Christmas tree in 1874.

   _____   _____

   _____   _____

Let's Write (and Draw a Picture)!

My favorite part of the story is when

_____

_____

_____

A Christmas Puzzle

If you look carefully at the word "Christmas," you will see the word "Christ." That is who Christmas is all about: Jesus Christ. John 3:16 says, "For God so loved the world, that He gave His only begotten Son, that whoever believes in Him should not perish, but have everlasting lif

C __ __ __ __ __   Jesus is also called _____

H __ __ __   God is _____ (perfect, sinless).

R __ __   A candy cane is _____ and white.

I __ __   Jesus was born in a stable because there was no room in the _ _____.

S __ __ __   The Wise Men followed this when they were looking for Jesus.

T __ __ __   We like to decorate this and hang lights and balls on it.

M __ __ __ __   Mary laid Jesus in a _____

A __ __ __ __ __   These heavenly beings told the shepherds the news about Jesus' birth.

S __ __ __   God sent Jesus to die for our _____

Color the picture.

The Magi Find Jesus

It took the Magi (the Wise Men) a long time to reach Bethlehem. But when they did, they worshiped the new King and brought him gifts: gold, frankincense, and myrrh.

Help the Magi find their way through this maze to the house where Baby Jesus and his family stayed. Do not cross any black lines.

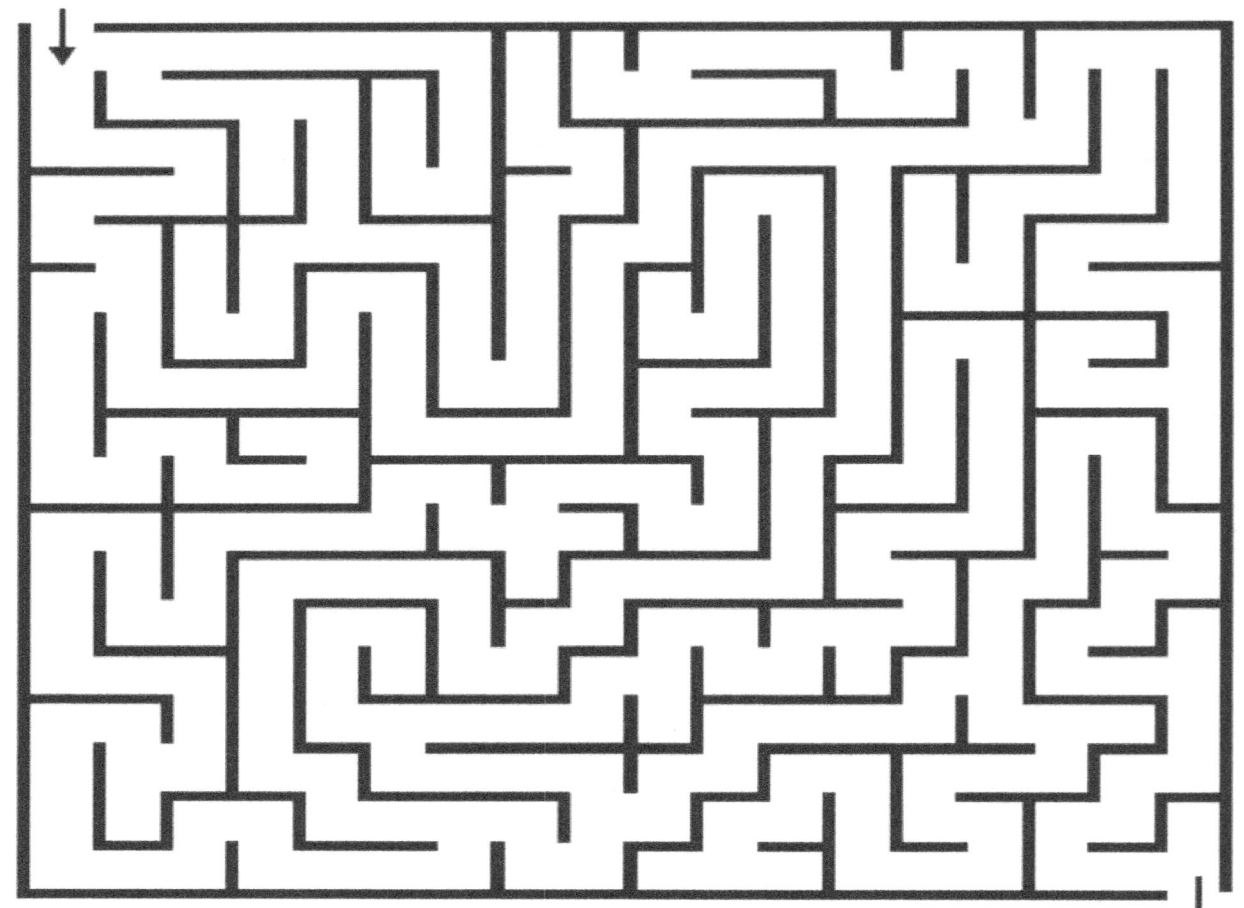

And they [the magi] came into the house and saw the Child with Mary His mother, and they fell down and worshiped Him; and opening their treasures they presented to Him gifts of gold and frankincense and myrrh." ~ Matthew 2:11

Victorian Christmas Decorations-Snowflakes

Children hung homemade decorations on the tree and in the house. They made colorful paper chains from strips of paper, looped and glued. They cut snowflakes. You need a scissors. Cut out the circles below (or use these circles as patterns on colored tissue paper.)

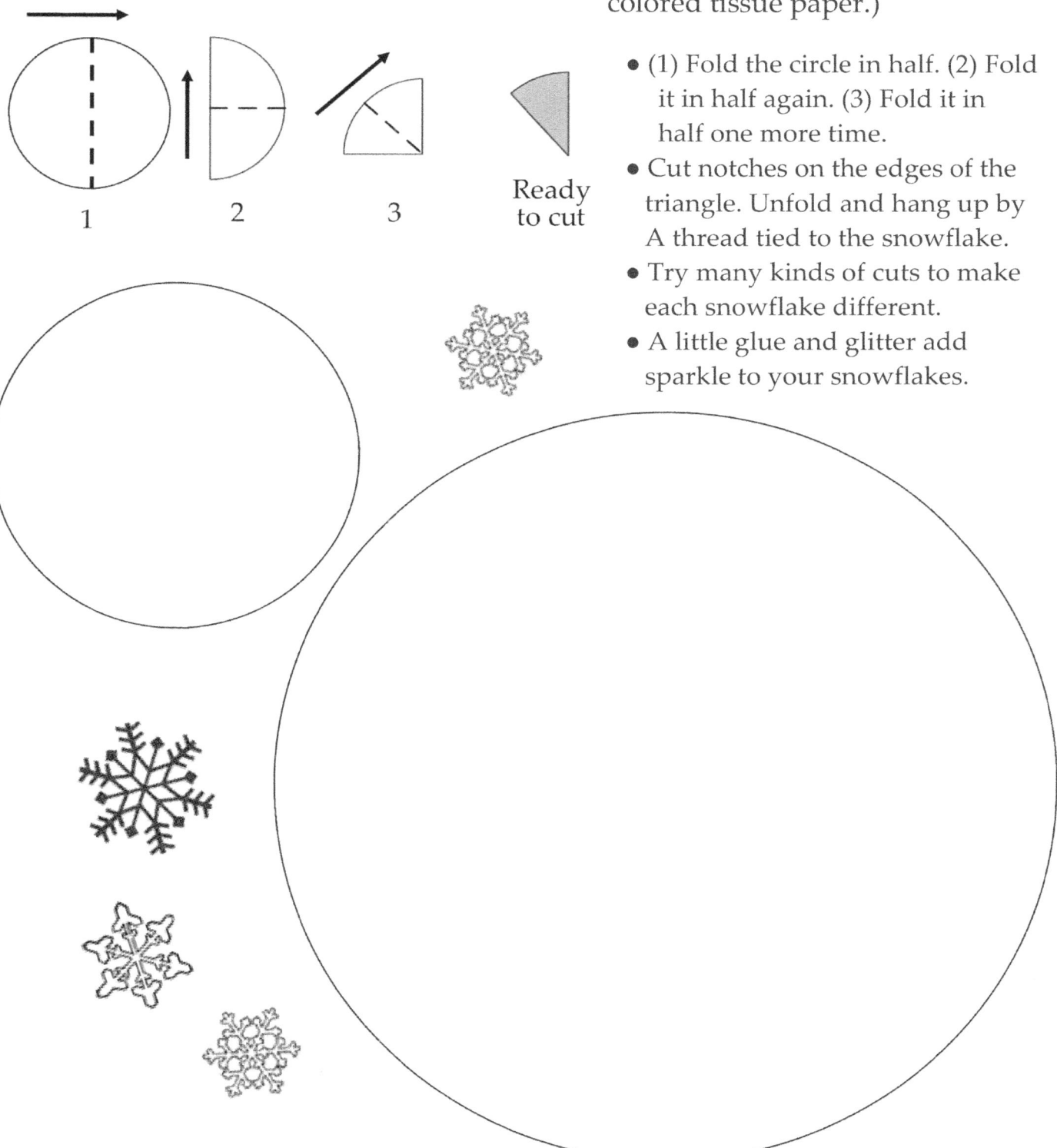

- (1) Fold the circle in half. (2) Fold it in half again. (3) Fold it in half one more time.
- Cut notches on the edges of the triangle. Unfold and hang up by A thread tied to the snowflake.
- Try many kinds of cuts to make each snowflake different.
- A little glue and glitter add sparkle to your snowflakes.

Character Trait – Joyful

Keeping a good attitude even when I am faced with unpleasant situations.

Joyful

Rejoice in the Lord always and again I say, rejoice.   Philippians 4:4

The Bible says to rejoice in the Lord *always*. It is easy for Andi to feel joyful when she is with Taffy and Riley. But she must also learn to be joyful when things are not going her way (like when Aunt Rebecca visits). God will work all things out for your good and His glory. Rejoice in the Lord!

Sometimes you (like Andi) must *choose* to be joyful, even when you feel upset or angry.

Thinking of ways that we can thank God for His gifts helps us stay joyful. In the box, draw something that makes you feel happy. Use it to remind you to rejoice in the Lord always.

Answer Key 1 – Andi's Pony Trouble

Page 7: Ch. 1–3
1. Andi
2. A
3. 6
4. May; 1874
5. Justin, Chad, Mitch, Melinda
6. Coco
7. a horse
8. NO
9. A
10. rooster
11. 18

Page 8: New Words for Chapters 1–3
See matching words answers on page 7 of the book.

1. scowled
2. pokey
3. hand-me-down
4. slumped
5. juggle

Page 12: Ch. 4-6
1. Riley
2. he chases her; he pecks her; he makes her spill her eggs; he is mean
3. 2
4. YES
5. Midnight
6. eight
7. brown
8. brown
9. NO
10. gallop
11. Coco's reins
12. C
13. YES

Page 13: New Words for Ch. 4-6
1.-3. See answers on page 7 of book.
4. bridle
5. tangled
6. trot
7. jack-in-the-box

Page 14: Color the Ponies
1. X
2. Color
3. Color
4. X
5. Color
6. X

Page 15: Egg math
1. 2 eggs
2. 31 chickens
3. 4 eggs
4. 8 eggs

Page 16: Measuring Midnight
1. 8 inches
2. 12 inches
3. 16 inches
4. 15 hands high

Page 17: Ch. 7–9
1. C
2. standing on Midnight
3. YES
4. B
5. Midnight
6. nobody
7. A
8. A-NO; B-NO
9. YES
10. Coco
11. happy

Page 18: New Words Chapters 7-9
1. B
2. C
3. A
4. B

Who Am I?
5. Justin
6. Melinda
7. Taffy
8. Riley
9. Coco
10. Chad
11. Mitch
12. Mother

Page 19: Maze

Page 20: Ch. 10 and Peek into the Past
1. check drawing
2. Chad
3. Taffy
4. white; white; gold
5. ~~car~~ horse buggy ~~bus~~ ~~truck~~ wagon ~~van~~ carriage

Page 21: Funny Ways to Talk
1. We are having a noisy rainstorm.
2. That was so easy!
3. You are grumpy this morning.
4. Slow down! Not so fast!
5. Something strange is going on around here.
6. You are in so much trouble!
7. Stop talking.
8. You act like you know everything.

Answers Key 2- Andi's Indian Summer

Page 25:
Chapters 1-3
1. B
2. Snowflake
3. NO
4. 10 cents
5. C
6. YES
7. Uncle Sid
8. A
9. B
10. Indians
11. Mitch
12. C
13. YES

Page 26: New Words Ch. 1–3
See matching words answers on page 7 of the book.

1. gasped   3. plopped
2. hollered   4. capture

Page 30: Ch. 4 –6
1. Taffy
2. "skin you alive"
3. He could ride an Indian pony, He could hunt with a bow
4. NO
5. C
6. YES
7. the creek
8. Her head hangs down, her tail droops
9. NO
10. a frog
11. C

Pages 32:
Mystery animal:
FROG

Page 31: New Words Ch. 4–6: Cookhouse
Crossed out words: ice cream sundaes, TV dinners, Hot Pockets, Popsicles
1. B   2. A   3. C   4. A   5. C

Page 37: Ch. 7-9
1. D
2. Indians
3. Andi
4. Midnight
5. NO
6. Yokut
7. Lum-pa
8. C
9. B
10. berries, acorns, shells, beads
11. rocks

Page 38: Yokut Word Puzzle
Y e l l e d
O h ó m
K i n d
U n c l e
T a f f y

I n s i d e
N o v e l
D a y
I c e
A c o r n s
N u t s
S u m m e r

Page 40: Ch. 10 & Peek into Past
1. Choo-nook
2. shell necklace
3. red
4. draw a horse
5. worked in factories, picked crops, took care of cows and sheep
6. YES

Pages 33 –35: Creek Animals
FISH: trout; minnow
INSECTS: water bug; mosquito; fly; dragonfly; bee
AMPHIBIANS: frog; salamander
REPTILES: snake; turtle
MAMMALS: deer; fox; bobcat; beaver

Page 41: Alike and Different

Venn diagram:
- **Choo-nook**: eats acorn mush*, wears a grass skirt, lives in a hut, makes baskets, lives by a creek, Indian girl
- **Both**: has long hair, loves to play, loves her family
- **Andi**: a white girl, has her own horse, lives in a big house, wears overalls, eats soup and bread, lives on a ranch

* This could be "both" since Andi ate the mush

Pages 43: Diligence
1. grateful   5. finish
2. work   6. complain
3. trust   7. obey
4. try   8. lazy

Answer Key 3 – Andi's Fair Surprise

Page 45: Ch. 1-3
1. Duke
2. A
3. NO
4. Chad
5. **Mother**: jars of jelly
   Chad & Mitch: cows and horses
   Melinda: a quilt
   Riley: Henry the rooster
   Andi: nothing
6. Chad
7. NO
8. Justin
9. bumps her nose, hat slips down, stomach feels sick
10. soot
11. Riley

Page 46: New words Ch. 1-3
See matching words answers on page 7 of book

1. spoiling
2. teasing
3. ruffled
4. patient
5. swayed

Page 50: Ch. 4-6
1. hotel (or bed)
2. one week
3. hat
4. A
5. B
6. 696
7. C
8. YES
9. horses, sheep, cows, chickens, pigs
10. Carrie
11. horse
12. lamb

Page 47: Where Is the State Fair?

CALIFORNIA
Sacramento
•FRESNO

Page 51: New Words Ch. 4-6
1.-3. See answers on page 7 of the book

4. menu
5. ticket
6. waitress
7. spinning wheel
8. tip

Page 52: Fair Animals Math
Horses: 32
Cows: 28
Pigs: 20
Chickens: 36
Sheep: 25
1. **chickens**
2. **pigs**
3. **five**

Page 53: Who am I?
1. rooster
2. rabbit
3. pig
4. turkey
5. sheep
6. goat
7. horse
8. hen
9. duck
10. cow
11. dog
12. cat

Page 54: Ch. 7-9
1. NO
2. pony
3. 20 cents
4. B
5. cowboy hat
6. C
7. third
8. A
9. Uncle Sid, Chad, other ranchers
10. Inky
11. YES
12. Melinda
13. Chad and Uncle Sid

Page 55: Twenty cents
16 cents
18 cents
15 cents
20 cents

Andi spends most of her money on the Ring Toss game.

Page 57: Ch. 10 and Peek into the Past
1. Carrie
2. C
3. cowboy hat
4. A
5. 1854
6. NO
7. Answers will vary.

Page 56: Rooster
—Henry the Eighth (rooster)
—Henry pecked the judge.

Page 61: "Security"
1. God, good
2. love
3. Shepherd
4. valley, evil
4. valley, evil
5. forever
6. people, pasture

* This could be "both" since Andi ate the

Answer Key 4 – Andi's Scary School Days

Page 63: Ch. 1-3
1. stall (or barn)
2. B
3. Riley
4. Justin
5. A
6. Mitch
7. YES
8. B
9. YES
10. Andrea
11. C

Page 63: New Words Ch. 1-3
See matching words answers on page 7 in the book.
1. squirmed   2. fuss   3. adorable   4. scolded   5. squished

Page 67: "America"
thee—an old-fashioned word that means "you"
liberty—freedom
Pilgrim—the people who came to America aboard the *Mayflower*
pride—when you feel good about doing something well

Page 65: Flag
1. 37 stars
2. 37 states
3. 13 stripes
4. 13 colonies
5. 50 stars
6. 50 states
7. 13 stripes

Page 66: Andi's schoolroom
—Andi's classroom holds <u>24</u> seats.

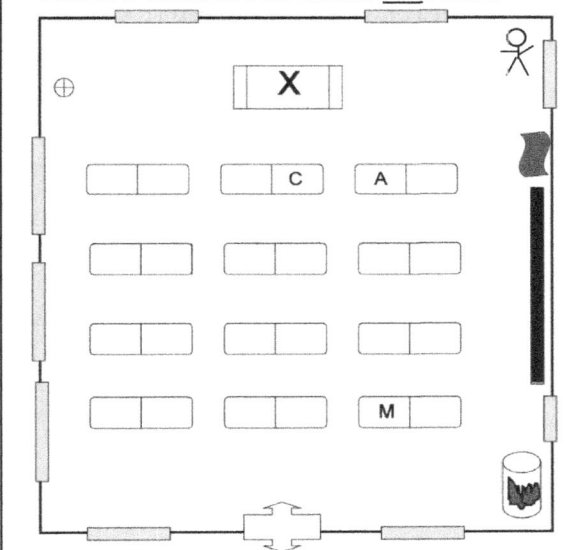

Page 68: Ch. 4-6
1. rat, fat, cat, sat
2. NO
3. C
4. Melinda
5. NO
6. Henry the Eighth
7. A
8. the snake rattle
9. Melinda
10. late
11. blue
12. Pickles
13. NO
14. the lizard

Page 69: New Words Ch. 4-6
See matching words answers on page 7 of the book.
1. punishment
2. jump rope
3. courthouse
4. snagged

Page 77: Ch. 7-9
1. under Andi's desk   7. C
2. Andi   8. YES
3. B   9. Cory's
4. NO   10. A
5. law office   11. Justin
6. ties a ribbon around him

Page 78: Fun with Words Ch. 7-9
1. The lizard zipped under the teacher's desk.
2. Andi sat as still as a fence post.
3. Andi looked up and down the busy street.
4. The horse backed up at her touch.
5. A large man stood right above her.

Page 79: Maze

Page 80: Ch. 10 & Peek into Past
1. God, Justin, Miss Hall
2. NO
3. ring the bell
4. read Bible; sang songs
5. 18 years old
6. 5 years old   7. 5, 7, 3

Page 83: "Peaceful"
1. a storm
2. the disciples
3. all people

Answer Key 5 - Andi's Lonely Little Foal

Page 85: Ch. 1-3
1. B
2. Answers will vary
3. Johnny
4. NO
5. NO
6. Melinda
7. 8 years, 6 years
8. C
9. YES
10. C
11. Prince, King, Duke
12. B
13. King

Page 86: New Words Ch. 1-3
1. nicker
2. nuzzled
3. A
4. B
5. A
6. C

Page 88: A Penny for Your Thoughts
1. D
2. E
3. A
4. C
5. F
6. H
7. B
8. G

Page 89: Lonely Foal maze

Page 90: Ch. 4-6
1. Yippee-ki-yay!
2. foot (or) hoof
3. A
4. Cook
5. NO
6. B
7. whinnies
9. apples, sugar, carrots
10. Chad (or) her brother
11. 11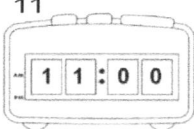

Page 91: New Words Ch. 4-6
See matching words answers on page 7 of the book

1. gulped
2. scrambled
3. heaps
4. rustled
5. cozy

Page 100: New Words Ch. 7-9
1. A
2. B
3. C
4. A
5. B
6. slingshot
7. bench
8. brandmark

Page 99: Ch. 7-9
1. Henry the Eighth (rooster)
2. ~~Johnny~~ the Bible story ~~leaving Taffy~~ the songs her Sunday school teacher ~~going to "school" on Sunday~~
3. "Jesus Loves Me"
4. YES
5. acorns
6. A
7. weaning
8. YES

Page 102: Ch. 10 & Peek into Past
1. C
2. Riley
3. NO
4. Sky
5. They slept in the bunkhouse, They worked hard, They fixed fences.

Page 103: "Boldness"
1. pray
2. playground
3. friends
4. faith
5. home
6. school
7. lie
8. steal

Answer Key 6 – Andi's Circle C Christmas

Page 105: Ch. 1-3
1. in the barn (hayloft)
2. Fly
3. YES
4. sling shot, harmonica, ~~doll~~, lasso, ~~hair ribbon~~, ~~new dress~~, knife, brush for Taffy
5. NO
6. Aunt Rebecca (old lady)
7. NO
8. Elizabeth
9. B
10. play with a boy, wear overalls, keep a lizard
11. C

Page 106: New Words Ch. 1-3
See matching words answers on page 7 of the book.
1. special
2. stuffed
3. invite
4. instant
5. thumping

Page 108: Where Is San Francisco?

Page 109: The Fort
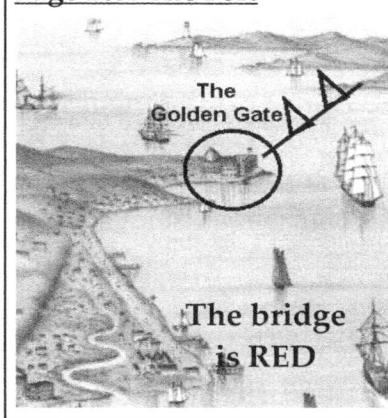
The bridge is RED

Page 110: Ch. 4-6
1. Justin
2. C
3. Aunt Rebecca's
4. A
5. OLDER
6. Andrea Rose Carter
7. Answers will vary.
8. D
9. lasso
10. pull a buggy

Page 111: New Words Ch. 4-6
1.-2. Answers on p. 7 book.
3. A
4. C
5. B
6. A
7. Draw a fence post.

Page 112: Story Characters
Andi—the main character in *Circle C Christmas*
Riley—Andi's friend, who lives on the ranch
Justin—Andi's oldest brother. He offers to cut up her meat.
Aunt Rebecca—Andi's grumpy aunt from San Francisco. She doesn't like spiders.
Chad—Andi's other big brother. He's bossy.
Taffy—Andi's foal
Coco—the pony Andi rides while wearing her new dress
Melinda—Andi's big sister. She helps Andi make a Christmas present for their mother
Uncle Sid—Riley's uncle; ranch foreman
Pickles—Andi's lizard. Eats spiders & flies.

Page 113: Ch. 7-9
1. B
2. spiders; 15
3. a jar
4. Mother
5. Mother & Rebecca Andi & Riley
6. NO
7. the wheel
8. Aunt Rebecca bumped her head, it's raining, Andi is cold and wet, it will be dark soon

Page 114: New Words Ch. 7-9
1.-2. see answers page 7 of book.
3. A
4. B
5. A
6. C
7. B

Page 115: What's Different?
1. no butterfly near Andi's arm
2. butterfly on tulip
3. no hair ribbon
4. egg basket
5. holding chicks
6. butterfly's shadow missing
7. frog hiding
8. missing flower blossom

Page 116: Ch. 10 & Peek into Past
1. she screams, she loses her hat, she gets wet
2. mud puddle
3. his mother
4. C
5. candles
6. Answers will vary.

Page 117 Puzzle
C hrist
H oly
R ed
S tar
T ree
M anger
A ngels
S ins

What's Next?

Andi continues her adventures on the Circle C ranch as a spunky nine-year-old in the brand-new Circle C Stepping Stones series. At long last, Taffy is old enough to ride, and Andi is ready for new, older adventures.

For readers ages 7-10.

Book 1: *Andi Saddles Up*

Book 2: *Andi Under the Big Top*

Book 3: *Andi Lassos Trouble*

Book 4: *Andi to the Rescue*

Book 5: *Andi Dreams of Gold*

Book 6: *Andi Far from Home*

The first activity guide is free at **CircleCBooks.com**

Or purchase the full workbook and lapbook(s).

For readers ages 9-13

Circle C Adventures

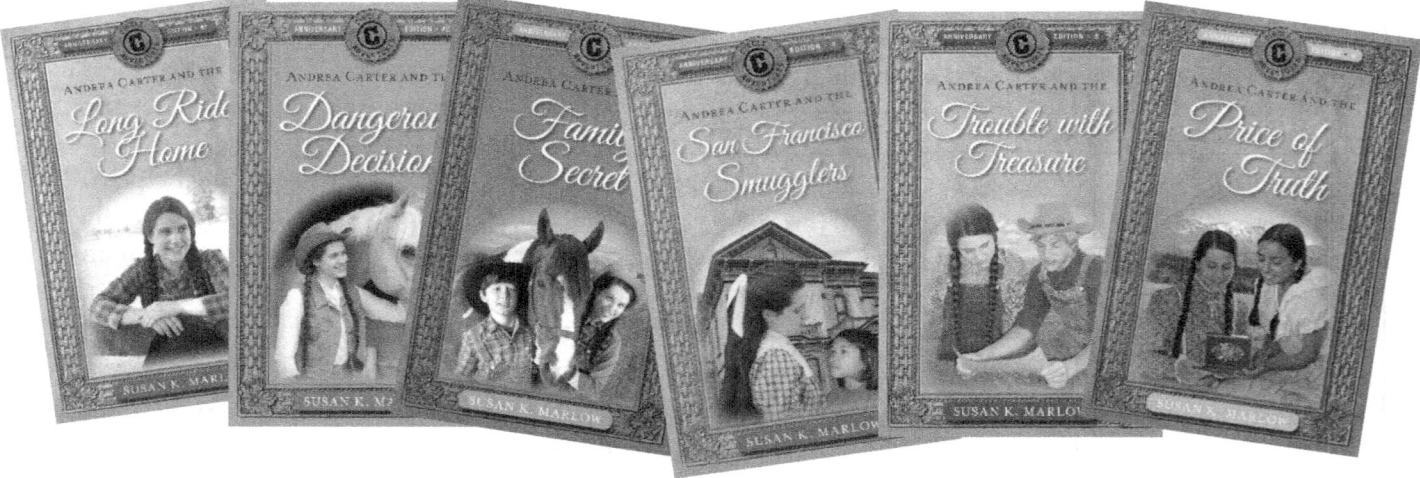

Each book features twelve-year-old Andi Carter and her palomino mare, Taffy. A free study guide for the first book, *Long Ride Home*, can be downloaded at:

CircleCBooks.com

Made in the USA
Monee, IL
29 May 2024

59082214R00072